MORE STUFF IRISH PEOPLE LOVE

Colin Murphy & Donal O'Dea

THE O'BRIEN PRESS
DUBLIN

First published 2012 by The O'Brien Press Ltd
12 Terenure Road East, Rathgar, Dublin 6, Ireland.
Tel: +353 1 4923333; Fax; +353 1 4922777
Email: books@obrien.ie; Website: www.obrien.ie

ISBN: 978-1-84717-355-3

A catalogue record for this title is available from The British Library

1 2 3 4 5 6 7 8
12 13 14 15 16 17

Cover design: Donal O'Dea
Cover image based on 'Mother Mary at Grotto' by Kitsen, courtesy of Dreamstime

Printed and bound in Spain by Imago.
The paper used in this book is produced using pulp from managed forests

Picture Credits:
page 39: Arron Roseberg; p47: Tom Creggan photographed by Joe Mabel; p49: Emmet Murphy; p59: Wendel Fisher; p67: Reproduced by kind permission of Inpho; p69: Mario Antonio Pena Zapateria; p84: Sean Rowe; p91: Softeis; p95: O'Dea; p97: Frederic Salein; p115: William Murphy; p116: Anthony McGuinness; p119: Donna Sheets; p121: Paddy Junki.

MORE STUFF IRISH PEOPLE LOVE

E
Du.

Colin Murphy is the co-author of thirteen humorous books in the *Feckin'* series about aspects of Irish culture, and *Stuff Irish People Love*, as well as *The Most Famous Irish People You've Never Heard Of,* which tells of Irish emigrants who found fame abroad but are little known in their homeland. Formerly the Creative Director of one of Ireland's leading advertising agences, he is now a full-time writer. His ambitions include climbing every mountain in Ireland and, more importantly, visiting every pub in Ireland. He lives in Dublin with his wife, Grainne, and their two children, Emmet and Ciara.

Donal O'Dea is the co-author, and illustrator, of thirteen humorous books in the *Feckin'* series about aspects of Irish culture, and *Stuff Irish People Love*. Currently the Creative Director of Owens DBB, one of Ireland's leading advertising agencies, he somehow finds time to manage a children's football team, compete in gruelling Alpine cycling challenges, write books and do the gardening, not to mention squeezing in frequent visits to O'Donoghue's in Baggot Street. Donal lives in Dublin with his wife, Karen, and their three children, Gavin, Leya and Alyson.

1 Packing the 'makings of a fry' to take on holiday.

As Irish people we enjoy mocking the prevalence of restaurants and bars in sunny holiday resorts that loudly advertise 'English Fish 'n Chips here!' written on a large British Union flag.

'I mean, for Jaysus' sake, what are the English like?' we tut-tut, and shake our heads despondently at our neighbours' lack of sophistication. Here they are, in Spain or Italy, home to an infinite variety of wonderful tapas or pasta dishes and wines to die for, and what do they do but sit around all day stuffing their faces with greasy, battered smoked cod and chips and quaffing pints of Carling Red Label? Having expressed our disgust and amusement at the sight, many of us Irish then promptly head back to our holiday apartments, dig out the Galtee rashers, Superquinn sausages and Clonakilty pudding (black and white) that we packed away with our knickers and jocks, and proceed to make a giant, greasy fry-up that we'll demolish on the balcony, accompanied by mugs of Barry's or Lyons tea, a box or two of which we also crammed in beside our sun tan lotion and bikinis. A few packs of Jacobs Mikado or Kimberley biscuits are also likely to have made the trip, and these will do nicely as dessert. We rationalise this behaviour by saying stuff like, 'Sure those Spanish sausages are bleedin' brutal,' or 'Where am I goin' te get black puddin' in feckin' Lanzarohee?' And who can argue with that?

But, unlike our English friends, we prefer to keep our little home food fetishes to ourselves, just so we can parade around foreign climes pretending we're well-travelled food sophisticates, and feeling superior. Later, of course, us and our other half will very likely proceed to the local hostelry where we will get completely rat-arsed. And sneaking into the 'Genuine English Takeaway' on the way home for a batterburger and chips is purely for medicinal reasons: 'Hey, Fiona, we'd better get some soakage or we'll be bleedin' despera with de hangovers tomorrow.' To which Fiona will reply: 'Yeah, we can make chip sambos. An' ye know, I tink I've still got some of dat Brennan's Batch Loaf left dat we packed in with de socks.'

Using tool metaphors.

'What are they on about?', you say. 'I *never* use tool metaphors'.

No? So you've never had a *rake* of drink, eh, ye dozy *spanner*? And don't try and claim that you've never told someone, most likely your kids, not to *shovel* their dinner into them. And talking of kids, those little *chisellers* do tend to *plough* through the money, don't they? Really, it's enough to make you want to go out tonight and get completely *hammered*.

Of course, the ultimate Irish tool metaphor is, well, 'tool' itself, which of course has two distinct meanings. The first is 'that crowd in the Dáil are

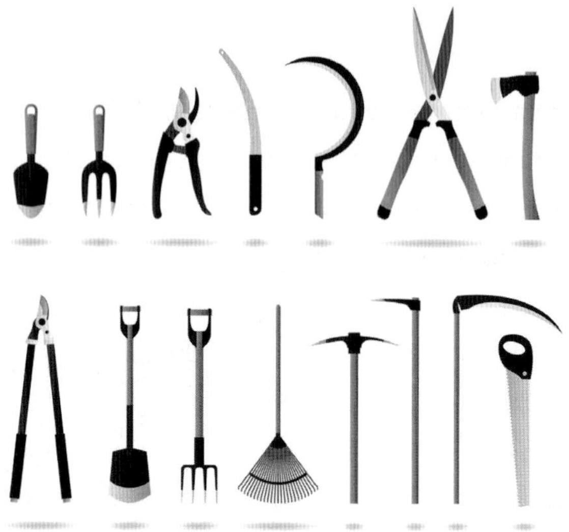

a right bunch of tools', which clearly in this case can have no meaning other than 'idiots'. And then there's the other version, its meaning self-evident in the ever popular phrase used by female members of Ireland's cultural elite: 'He has a tool on him as long as a well-hung donkey on Viagra.'

Singing 'Olé Olé Olé' to support Irish teams in any sport.

Now here's an interesting thought for those countless Irish football (and other sporting disciplines) supporters who love to chant 'Olé Olé Olé' whenever an Irish player manages to get a touch of the ball. Besides the fact that it is more commonly associated with bullfighting, one theory on the true origin of the word 'Olé', is that it is a corruption of the Arabic invocation of 'Allah', which was repeated over and over in praise of the Muslim God, i.e. 'Allah! Allah! Allah!'

The very notion of this might send the few fanatical Irish Catholics that are left scurrying to confession in search of absolution for inadvertently worshipping the god of another religion, as of course they know with absolute, one hundred percent certainty that they alone worship the one true God.

But we digress. Back to 'Olé', which some Irish fans probably believe is the brand name of the face cream their missus keeps in the cupboard in the jacks, while others mistakenly think it is a bullfighting chant. But, apparently, it originated, at least in a sporting context in, surprise, surprise, Spain, back in the 1980s after Real Sociedad had won La Liga. Their fans started chanting '*Campeones, campeones, **hobe, hobe, hobe***'. *Hobe* is Basque, (we looked this up) which means 'We are the best'. This itself was misunderstood in wider Spain to mean 'Oé Oé Oé', as in '*A por ellos, oé*' which approximates as 'Here we go', and if you listen carefully when watching a Spanish football match, this is what the fans are chanting, and not 'Olé' (which means 'bravo'), so, in effect, we are chanting a word that is probably an incantation to Allah and in a sporting context is a misinterpretation of a misinterpretation of a word that has nothing to do with football, and certainly nothing to do with Irish football!

However, as Wikipedia notes, 'Olé Olé Olé' has been '*appropriated by the supporters of the Republic of Ireland national football team*.' This is inaccurate, as it has also been appropriated by supporters of Irish camogie teams, rugby teams, boxing teams, synchronised swimming teams and even Irish cricket teams. And while it's sort of a shame that we couldn't have come up with a chant that had some authentic Irish connection, you have to admit that 'Olé Olé Olé's' Irish equivalent isn't quite as catchy: '*Ar aghaidh linn*', '*Ar aghaidh linn*'.

Moving Statues.

When Ballinspittle in County Cork launched the phenomenon of the 'moving statue' onto the world stage back in the innocent days of 1985, the BBC's 'Newsnight' programme reported that over a quarter of a million people had visited the site within weeks of the apparent visitation by the Virgin Mary. Little did we know then, but Ballinspittle was just the first stop on a nationwide tour of Ireland that the Blessed Virgin had embarked upon, clashing with several boy bands who had the same idea. Watching that BBC report (it is available on YouTube) in post-fundamentalist-Catholic Ireland, one might be struck by a nagging suspicion, despite the relative respect paid by the BBC reporter, that at any moment he might burst into hysterical laughter. And

who could blame him? We all look back now ourselves and snigger, but the sniggers weren't that prevalent at all back in the 1980s, and there are many among us still who would be reluctant to admit that they gave the possibility of a miracle serious consideration. Yes, we as a people were that pathetic. Of course, during the Nineties and Noughties, we largely abandoned our spiritual beliefs in favour of worshipping easy money, and did so with equal fervour as those Ballinspittle devotees, once again proving what a gullible, easily-led bunch of gobshites we are!

For those too young to recall the strange event(s), here's a quick guide. In July 1985, a group of thirteen worshippers were making their regular visit to the Ballinspittle shrine to the Virgin Mary, when one of them noticed that the statue was breathing, and several of the others saw that the statue's hands were moving, (whether they were waving, clapping, twiddling, wiggling or drumming their fingers was never clarified). Unlike most people who, faced with an apparently inanimate object springing to life, would leg it like the bejaysus, this group interpreted the painted plaster statue's movement as a visitation by the Virgin Mary and rejoiced, then hastily reported it to all and sundry. The Irish people, then as now in the grip of a deep recession, descended on Ballinspittle in their droves, perhaps in search of a spiritually uplifting experience to ease their gloom, perhaps in search of a job in the now-thriving local tourist economy. Not to imply that the entire thing was a clever marketing ploy by the local Chamber of Commerce, as nobody doubts the word or self-belief of the original witnesses any more than they doubt the self-belief of the Yaohnanen tribe on the South Pacific island of Tanna, who heartily believe that Britain's Prince Philip is a divine being.

But, before you could say a decade of Hail

Marys and a few Our Fathers, reports of other moving statues were pouring in from all over the country, testifying to the fact that the Virgin Mary was on a nationwide tour. Statues were leaping into life at a phenomenal rate in Kerry, Kilkenny, Waterford, Mayo, Tipperary etc, and, not content just to move, they had now added bleeding, hovering and crying to their list of startling abilities. People everywhere waited with bated breath for the first report of a Virgin Mary break-dancing or even perhaps giving a rousing rendition of 'She Moved through the Fair'.

There were also, it must be noted, sceptics. But by then Ireland had embraced the moving statue so much (and possibly been embraced back) that these were dismissed as atheistic crackpots. Scientific explanations offered included the possibility of Mary's halo of electric lights in the darkness creating the illusion of movement, the power of mass suggestion, the auto kinetic effect, and lastly, the people of Ireland being completely bonkers.

One might think that in these (so-called) more enlightened times, the phenomenon of the moving statue has moved on (ha ha), but within the last decade the BBC and RTÉ were back to record documentaries about the episode and many of the Ballinspittle locals still stand by their stories, including a former Garda sergeant who claimed the statue became airborne.

Meanwhile, back on planet Earth, there is much talk during the present recession of people flocking back to churches to renew the faith they had abandoned in exchange for filthy, borrowed lucre during the Celtic Tiger years, so the possibility exists that we may soon have another crazy summer of statue-shifting. You read it here first.

But the last word goes to the Dublin wit who, during the summer of 1985, left a sign hanging around a statue of the Virgin Mary in Sandymount reading: 'Out of Order'.

Saying 'Jaysus!'.

Originally a word of Dublin origin, 'Jaysus!', like the Virgin Mary in the previous piece, has been on the move and nowadays is often heard exclaimed loudly in towns and

villages from Donegal to Wexford, or wherever an Irish person witnesses a politician being truthful about his or her expenses. Like several other uniquely Irish slang words, we like to say '*Jaysus*!' to distinguish ourselves from the international standard form of taking the Lord's name in vain of '*Jesus*!' or '*Jesus Christ*!' This is not only a statement of our Irishness, but also, despite our professed overcoming of Catholic guilt, we still feel that '*Jaysus*!' isn't *really* blasphemous, whereas '*Jesus*!' might just be a venial sin.

Some local variations include 'Holy Jaysus', 'Be da Jaysus' and 'Jaysus, Mary and Joseph'.

The word 'Jaysus' actually operates in a similar way to the word 'feck' in that it is a polite form of that other word that earned you a clatter if you said it when you were a kid. Which allows us Irish to make potentially very profane statements such as 'Feckin' Jaysus', without offending anyone.

Not protesting about anything.

Imagine the scenario where a bunch of foreigners arrive in a country and starts dictating what the State can and cannot spend, orders them to slash this and that, and at the same time pay enormous amounts of their money to faceless punters who gambled vast sums of dosh on shares that dive-bombed.

Imagine this country already had a bunch of corrupt, incompetent, power-hungry politicians running the place who didn't give a fiddler's about its own people and swanned around in limousines and paid themselves ginormous wages and bonuses and allowed the financiers and civil servants who had banjaxed the country also to be paid humungous wads of cash, not to mention mind-bogglingly large bonuses and pensions. And then, even when that lot were thrown out of government, the next lot simply carried on kow-towing to their foreign masters at the expense of the people. Surely such a scenario would prompt demonstrations, riots and mayhem on a massive scale? No?

No.

Welcome to Ireland.

We don’t do protests. At least not like other countries do. Sure, there have been a few demonstrations here and there, like the senior citizens, the bunch of new wave eejits in Dame Street and a handful of people waving signs about smelly septic tanks, but, generally speaking, when it comes to protesting, we’re as useless as a one-armed man in a rope-climbing competition. As austerity struck in countries all over Europe, the Greeks, the Spanish, the Portuguese and the French all took to the streets in their millions, sometimes having the proverbial shite kicked out of them by baton-wielding policemen. But did that stop them? No, they were back for more and more, often surrounding the offending government and financial institutions and terrifying the crap out of the cowering sleeveens inside. What did we do? We sat in our armchairs and pubs and moaned about things being ‘a disgrace’ and said stuff like 'Those feckers should be put in jail'. That's about it. Our country destroyed for a generation and all we can muster are a few groans, a few letters to the paper and a few outraged calls to 'Liveline'.

So what's behind the perverse love we have of letting the offending officials away with blue murder without so much as a peep? For one thing, we're an awful lazy bunch of head-the-balls. We just couldn't be arsed. Anyway, somebody else should be out protesting, we think. Then there's the historical thing that supposedly we're so used to being trodden on and there's nothing we can do about it. And, of course, we've become the most cynical nation on earth. We trust nobody and suspect everyone is either lying or in it for whatever he/she can get out of it. If Daniel O'Connell, Jesus Christ, Ghandi, Michael Collins, Mother Teresa and Nelson Mandela suddenly materialised and announced they were going to lead a mass protest in O'Connell Street tomorrow, we'd all furrow our brows and wrinkle our noses in suspicion and say something like 'Those feckers are up to no good. Maybe they've got a book deal or something.

C'mon, let's go for a pint.'

Perversely, we've begun to wear our love of inaction like a badge of pride. We've even fooled ourselves into believing that our European neighbours admire us for it, when in fact they're rolling in the aisles at our willingness to be trodden upon.

And people wonder how the Brits managed to repress us for 750 years!

Really, you, the reader, should start a protest movement about our inability to protest.

'I will in me arse', says you.

Putting the 'messages' in the 'press'.

For the benefit of our foreign readers, if an Irish person informs you that he/she has to run out to do a few 'messages', do not interpret this to mean that they've gone off to send a few private texts. Nor does it mean that they have to hand-deliver scribbled bits of paper to various people. In Ireland 'messages' loosely means 'groceries', shopping in

general, or it can mean personal business to carry out, such as having an eye test, visiting one's accountant or having a rectal scan. Having done the few 'messages', if these *do* happen to be groceries, the Irish person will return home and place their 'messages' in the 'press'.

This often prompts foreigners to imagine all Irish homes equipped with a strange contraption resembling an apple press with a giant handle on the top, which, when turned, crushes the person's tins of beans and jars of marmalade in some weird Irish ritual. Not so. We may be weird in many ways, but not that weird. A 'press' is simply an Irish name for a cupboard.

The etymology of 'press' is most likely that it comes from the Irish word *prios*, which means, surprise, surprise, 'cupboard'. The origin of 'messages' is less clear, although the word suggests that in the days before mass communication, Irish people tended to exchange information while visiting their local shop or village, where various messages vital to the functioning of the community would be exchanged, such as 'Make sure ye tell Kathleen and Mary that that little slut Bridget O'Connor is after gettin' herself pregnant', or 'I hear Paddy Joe's up to his arse in debt, drank it all away, so they say, the durty little sleeveen.'

8 Ignoring pedestrian crossing signals.

When a continental European person approaches a pedestrian crossing, he or she will dutifully stop, press the button and wait for the little green man and the funny electronic beeping sound to say that it is safe to cross. Our German or Belgian friends will do this irrespective of whether there are fifty juggernauts hurtling past in either direction or if the road

is entirely free of traffic in either direction as far as the eye can see.

You can just hear the Irish people howling with laughter at the very notion of doing this. The thought of standing still at the side of the road while the street is devoid of traffic is so alien to the Irish psyche that we consider anyone who does it to be either blind, having some form of 'turn', or suffering from a debilitating mental illness. Even when the road is busy, it is considered distinctly un-Irish to wait for the green man. To an Irish person, a speeding lorry, six cars, a couple of motor bikes and multiple cyclists is not considered a danger, it is considered a challenge, and it is every Irish man and woman's national duty to accept the gauntlet that has been thrown down and dodge their way to the other pavement in one piece.

In the U.S. tens of thousands of people are fined every year for so-called 'jaywalking', and the fines can be as much as $750. Guess how many Irish people are fined annually for similar offences? Well, it's roughly the same as the number of bankers who have been imprisoned for bankrupting Ireland.

It has often been said that Irish children get mixed messages from their parents, e.g. Irish Dads swilling from cans of lager while telling their kids they should never drink; Irish Mammies warning their kids through a cloud of exhaled carcinogenic fog that smoking will kill them etc. But this is most evident in our love of death-dodging on the public highways. First we fill our little darlings' heads with all sorts of sensible advice about looking left, right, left again, watching for the green man or waiting for the lady with the lollipop sign. We even teach them catchy little songs like 'The Safe Cross Code' (remember that one?) so that they'll never forget a word of this vital road safety advice. Then we're out shopping with them and we come to a pedestrian crossing. The child will stop as dutifully as a guide dog, only to have his little arm almost yanked from its socket as his mother hauls the bewildered and petrified little tot into a torrent of blaring traffic.

In Ireland, when we approach a pedestrian crossing on a chaotically busy street, we don't see a little red man, we see a sign saying something like: 'You gotta ask yourself one question – do ya feel lucky, *punk*?'

9 The Little Black Babies.

Ireland's youth, naturally, won't have a clue what the 'Little Black Babies' were, but anyone over forty will probably have a pretty clear memory of bringing their few meagre pennies to school every week to help save a Little Black Baby. Way back in the distant days of the Sixties and Seventies, Irish Catholic schools were each equipped with a little statue made of plaster, depicting a tiny black African child kneeling in prayer. There was a slot (was it in his head or in the attached box?) and every time a coin was dropped in, the little fella's head would rock back and forth as though he was nodding his thanks. These statues were officially known as 'Sammys' (we're not making this up). Yes, it all sounds so iffy now and politically incorrect, but Sammy represented all the

Little Black Babies that our contributions were saving, not just from starvation and disease in Africa, but also from eternal damnation. How we loved our Little Black Babies and the notion that we were saving these poor unfortunates from the flames of hell.

The money actually went to something known as 'The Missions', which we vaguely understood as a region of the Dark Continent populated by jolly red-faced Irish priests from Ballygobackwards who always dressed in white robes as they did battle with Satan for the souls of the innocent, heathen black-skinned babies.

Some of our Christian Brother schoolteachers often gave the impression that if we contributed enough pennies, some day our own personal Black Baby would grow up and visit us in Ireland, and if our Little Black Baby was really lucky, we were told, he or she might have grown up to be a priest or a nun themselves. Wow.

There was even a scheme where kids who made extra contributions would get to give a Christian name to these ignorant, pagan black babies. And even today there are men and women in their forties and fifties in places like Mozambique or Uganda who are scratching their heads and wondering why they have names like Seamus Paddy Guebuza or Biddy Fionnuala Mbabazi.

Singing our party piece at a hooley.

You know the scene. After a celebration of some description, and usually when the barman has expelled the drunken revellers from the pub, everyone legs it back to someone's gaff so that the craic can continue long into the small hours. There's great banter going on and you can hardly hear yourself with the laughter and

talk, and then from somewhere in the room there emerges this hideous whining sound that could only have been born in the deepest bowels of hell itself. It grows in intensity and loudness, quickly silencing the chatter and sending the dog scurrying behind the sofa. Yes, you guessed it: your Uncle Mick has started singing 'Danny Boy'. The only problem is that he's actually singing it to the tune of 'Mursheen Durkin' and it emerges not as 'Oh Danny Boy, the pipes the pipes are calling' but as 'Ogghh Dsany Byyyy de pihpesss de fipess arrr crawlin'. After Uncle Mick has tortured poor Danny Boy to a slow, horrible death, the baton is passed to your granny, who enthusiastically launches into 'Come Back Paddy Reilly to Ballyjamesduff'. Unfortunately, her rendition is reminiscent of the sounds a hyena makes when put to death with a blow-torch. The enthusiasm grows as each in turn takes up the challenge, and we are treated to the sound of 'The Rose of Tralee' being strangled, 'Lanigan's Ball' being crushed to a bloody pulp, and 'The Jolly Beggar' begging for mercy.

Ah yes, we do love an oul' sing song, but unfortunately by the time all the whiskey in the jar has been drunk and the dawning of the day comes round, Irish eyes are definitely not smiling, not to mention our ears.

Your mother reproaching you for not knowing the names of your distant cousins' wives and kids.

Irish Mammies are famed for their uncanny ability to remember the names not just of everyone on every branch of the family tree, but even those clinging to the tiniest twig at the end of a distant limb. What purpose this ability serves is anyone's guess, but Irish Mammies do love to brandish their knowledge as though they were sacred chroniclers who had been appointed by some mysterious higher power to guard the treasures of family lore. This usually manifests itself something like this:

Mammy: 'I hear Patricia just had a new baby.'

Son/Daughter: 'Who's Patricia?'

Mammy pulls a startled face and then appears affronted by your ignorance.

Mammy: 'Who's Patricia? Patricia! Your cousin's wife in Leitrim.'

Son/Daughter: 'I have a cousin in Leitrim?'

Mammy: 'Your cousin Colm. What sort of an eejit

have I rared at all?'

Son/Daughter tries to rustle up some distant memory of a Colm, but fails. The blank look on his/her face prompts further irritation from Mammy, as she explains, with an exasperated, pained expression, the familial connections.

Mammy: 'Lord and Mary Mother of God, Joseph and all the saints save us. Colm is your third cousin, whose father is Mick, your second cousin who's married to that one Deirdre from Cork. Mick's mother, Fiona, who's from Ballybofey, is your first cousin, but she's a lot older than you on account of she was first born and you were last born, so she's old enough to be your granny. Her father was Seamus, your Da's eldest brother, but he's long since in the ground, his liver packed in, too fond of the drink that fella was. Now do you remember Patricia? Nice looking girl, but a bit flighty for my taste.'

You appear to be pondering, striving to remember, but actually you're contemplating matricide. Finally your Mammy throws her hands up in the air and walks away, as though you're a lost cause.

Mammy: 'You should be ashamed of yourself,

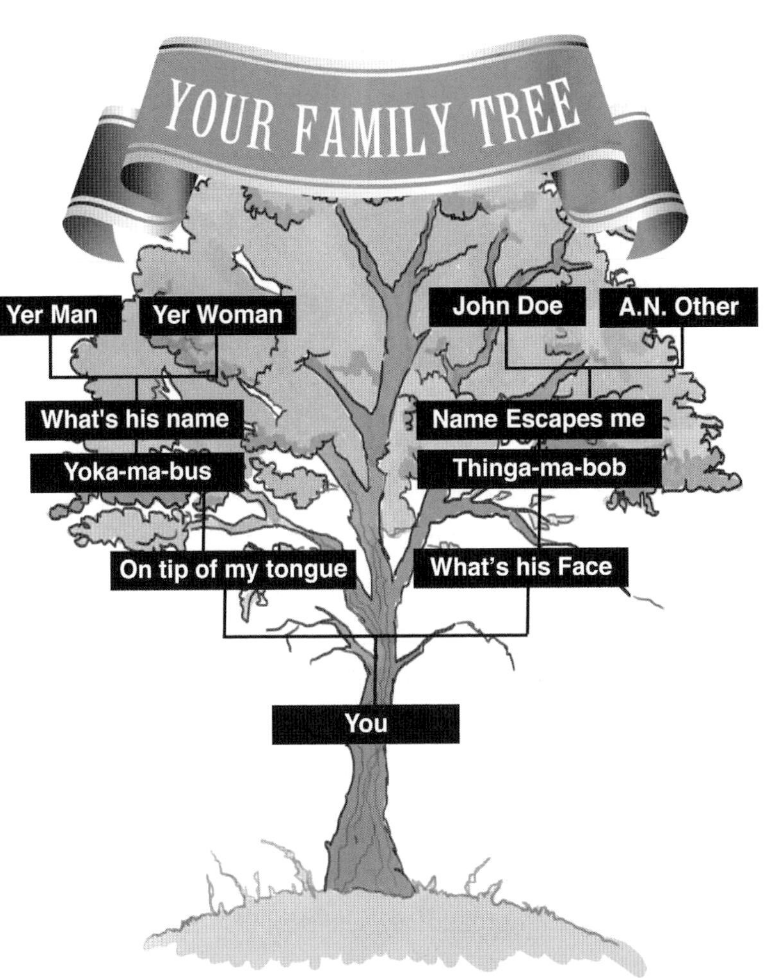
YOUR FAMILY TREE
Yer Man
Yer Woman
John Doe
A.N. Other
What's his name
Name Escapes me
Yoka-ma-bus
Thinga-ma-bob
On tip of my tongue
What's his Face
You

not knowing your family. Oh heaven help me, where on earth did I go wrong?'

You then make a secret pact with yourself to kill every last one of your cousins the length and breadth of Ireland.

12 Deliberately not pronouncing our 'th's.

Whenever an English person is telling a story or joke concerning an Irishman, as a means of trying to impart an Irish accent he usually lays heavy emphasis on our reluctance to pronounce the letters 'th'. The story will go something like this: '…so there's this 'orrible 'airy Irishman who lives in an 'aunted 'ouse in 'ampstead. But 'e never pronounces his 'th's, this Irishman, says 'tirty tree and a turd', 'e does, right 'eadcase 'e is….' All of which he and his mates will find uproariously hilarious. Our good friends in England being the easily amused race that they are, the irony of their own misplaced 'h's' entirely lost on all present.

Of course there are lots of reasons why we don't pronounce our 'th's' in certain situations, mostly relating to our switch over from speaking Irish to English and importing pronunciations and constructions when we did. But more to the point, why on earth would we try to pronounce certain words 'properly' when it involves such an effort. I mean, for Jaysus' sake, saying 'th' requires you to stick your tongue between your teeth and expel a short sharp puff of air just to say one lousy letter. Life's too short.

On top of which, most foreign people find our lovely, melodious accent really attractive and sexy, if often utterly incomprehensible, and Irish men will swear blindly that it significantly increases their chances of getting a pretty European girl into the sack: word has it that all you have to do is merely whisper something like 'I tink termodynamics are trilling', and Helga from Helsinborg or Frieda from Frankfurt will be eager to bear your children.

All of which is why we will continue proudly to neglect our 'th's', and leave our English friends to stumble and stutter their way through their sentences, while we charm the pants off the rest of the world.

Brides & grooms going to bed at 6am.

Traditionally, in most countries after the wedding ceremony and all the celebrations had reached their zenith at about 11pm, the guests would form a long archway with their arms, under which the happy couple would pass to loud and raucous cheering, after which they would proceed directly to the honeymoon suite for a night of unbridled passion. As most Irish couples live together nowadays before they're married, or certainly have long since indulged in a bit of hanky panky/jiggery-pokery/funky chicken, the desire to rush off to the bedroom and tear each other's clothes off for some more horizontal refreshment isn't as all-consuming as it might once have been. In other countries they usually go and attempt it anyway,

as it is expected of them. In Ireland, newlyweds take a slightly different approach. Having waved their goodbyes and thank yous, they go to the bedroom, change into some casual clothes and re-emerge in the reception room, where they proceed to get plastered and enjoy the craic until 6am, the thinking being that since they paid for the whole thing, why should they miss out on the biggest party they'll ever attend? Finally, having sat with friends and family exchanging amusing anecdotes and jokes until the sun comes up, the pair will once again say their farewells and make their way on very wobbly legs to the honeymoon suite, which cost €500 a night and in which, thus far, they have spent all of ten minutes, where they will indulge in a little romantic foreplay before suddenly collapsing unconscious and at right angles to each other on the gigantic bed, finally being woken by housekeeping at about 2pm the following day.

Both will, naturally, have insanely brutal hang-overs and be in such a foul mood that they'll spend the first full day of their marriage snapping at each other. Which is why the Irish approach to weddings is such a rewarding experience, as it provides the bride and groom with a wonderful foretaste of what the next fifty years will be like.

Never letting the truth get in the way of a good story.

Mark Twain was reputed to have coined the phrase 'Never let the truth get in the way of a good story', but surely he was thinking of us Irish when he uttered his remark, as, boy, do we love

to 'enrich' our telling of tales by the occasional 'exaggeration'. In fact, we Irish tend to think of the truth as a poor, lonely soul, lost and adrift on an empty sea, which is therefore constantly in need of company and cheering up.

Take the following example:

'Kevin went to the pub with his girlfriend Ailish, where he had one too many, tripped and cut his forehead, which required three stitches.'

The above simple tale is recounted in the village local the following Friday:

'Did ye hear Kevin Mulcahy is gay? Yeah, he came out to Ailish Flanagan, his girlfriend, in Murphy's Bar the other night and she skulled him with a bottle. He needed twelve stitches and then Ailish got off with Mick Tracy just to annoy him.'

By Saturday the tale has morphed into:

'Did you hear Kevin Mulcahy was snogging some gay fella in the jacks in Murphy's Bar and his girlfriend Ailish caught them and battered him with the leg of a chair? Needed surgery he did, and Kevin's sister, Tracey, attacked her with a bottle and she needed twelve stitches and then they were both arrested.'

By the time the tale has done the rounds of all the pubs in the locality, Kevin has been transformed into a sexual deviant who has now been reduced to a babbling idiot as a result of the violent assault by his drunken sister, Tracey, who herself is a couple of pints short of a milk churn, and who had always had a lesbian crush on Kevin's girlfriend, Ailish, who was into weird satanic rituals, but she's been arrested now for selling cocaine to small children.

And poor Kevin and Ailish wonder why people are looking at them funny in Mass on Sunday morning.

Still, you have to admit, Kevin's sexual preferences, Ailish's evil secrets and Tracy's lesbian tendencies is a much more interesting version than 'Kevin bumped his head in the pub.'

Winston Churchill once said that the truth was incontrovertible.

In Ireland's case, truth is not incontrovertible, it's convertible.

15 Driving indefinitely on a learner's permit.

Isn't it amazing that in this day and age there are people in Ireland in their seventies who are driving on our roads with just a learner's permit. What's wrong with that, you ask? Well, nothing, except that they actually got their original learner's permit or provisional licence when the Beatles were at Number 1 with 'Eleanor Rigby'. To use a medical metaphor, this is the equivalent of allowing a budding doctor perform a kidney transplant on you after he's passed his secondary school biology test. You see, there is no upper limit to the number of times you can obtain a new licence, as long as you complete a driving test every two years. But the legislators have missed one subtle flaw in this system – THE GOBSHITES KEEP FAILING THE TEST AGAIN AND AGAIN, SO THEY MUST BE BLEEDIN' BRUTAL DRIVERS!

So, basically, Ireland's roads are awash with eejits who don't know left from right, who believe brakes are for wimps and who really think it was considerate of the car manufacturer to put in that mirror for shaving/doing your make-up.

And as for the rule that says a person with two years' driving experience must accompany learner permit holders? What rule, one can hear them say. 'Sure that'd be terrible inconvenient altogether. Ye mean, me Ma or me Da is supposed to come with me if I want to drive te de pub for a few pints? Will ye go an' ask me arse!'

Yes, these are the kinds of people who are out there on Irish roads right now. So here's a safety tip for our foreign visitors thinking of hiring a car in Ireland. Take the train.

16 Eating all sorts of strange yokes.

The first 'Stuff' book dealt with a variety of strange foodstuffs beloved of the Irish race, such as Tayto Crisp sambos, ice cream in fizzy orange and Marietta biscuits stuck together with butter. Further research has uncovered even more of these culinary delights. Among the most popular were salad cream sandwiches – not yer fancy mayonnaise stuff – but Chef Salad Cream, and nothing else. Another favourite sambo was made with something called 'Sandwich Spread' (still available, although most of the jars on the supermarket shelves have been there since Dev died). This was a mixture of salad cream and Jaysus knows what else, but they looked like little bits of green, red and orange vegetables. This had one great thing going for it in the Irish household – it was CHEAP. Other cheap sambo favourites included those made with tinned picnic ham, which when blended into a bunch of lettuce leaves could be served up as a fancy 'salad'.

For those with a sweet tooth, but who also require their desserts to cost less than a single jelly bean, there's always 'Goody'. This treat was made of the stale bread left at the bottom of the Johnston Mooney and O'Brien bread wrapper, which was boiled in milk with a few spoons of sugar and a pinch of cinnamon thrown in. The resulting mess, resembling something a wild goat has vomited, was served up to delighted children all over the country, the poor little buggers not knowing any better. The name is ironic, one supposes.

Gur cake is another uniquely Irish delight. The name apparently comes from the old Irish schoolboy phrase 'to go on the gur', which means to go mitching from school. To provide their nutritional needs during their illicit day of getting up to no good, the mitchers would buy the cheapest, sweetest and most filling thing available, which happened to be this particular cake, thus giving rise to the term. This also evolved into the term 'gurriers'. Bet you didn't know that, eh?

The reason Gur cake was cheap was that at the end of the day in the bakery, the owner noticed that a lot of crap had accumulated around the floor during the day's work, so he told the bakers to sweep up all the oul' shite and make something with it so he could get even richer. So the original Gur cake most likely contained trampled fruit, dirty flour, mice droppings, splinters and a few cigarette butts. Even so, it tasted bleedin' deadly!

Our 700 years of oppression.

Despite our very friendly relations with our British neighbours in recent times, Irish people still love to trot out the old '700 years of oppression' every now and then to demonstrate what a poor downtrodden people we are, who, despite it all, have risen above the brutal persecution to build a nation free to repeatedly elect whatever bunch of corrupt sleeveens we want into government. Actually, the '700' years is inaccurate for a start, as we can pinpoint the moment our unfortunate relationship with our neighbours began to 1 May 1167 when the Normans arrived, and, if we take the official handover of power to the Irish Provisional Government in Dublin Castle on 16 January 1922, then what we should really be shouting about is 754 years, 8 months and 15 days of oppression, which is even better in terms of its

'poor us' quotient.

But we should get a couple of things straight. First of all, we actually *invited* the British, or rather Norman, hordes over here. Or at least Diarmuid Mac Murrough did, who was the King of Leinster, as he wanted help from King Henry II to get his kingdom back. But you know the way you invite someone to dinner and you can't get rid of them until 3am? Well, unfortunately, Diarmuid's guests decided to stay for seven and a half centuries. But the other thing that we should remind Republican fanatics who traditionally make much mileage out of the '700 years of British oppression' of is that the Normans were mostly French. Admittedly, the English did arrive not long after, and as we all know, didn't exactly endear themselves to the locals in subsequent centuries. But they did leave us one enduring legacy – the opportunity to portray ourselves as a wretched, long-suffering, hapless people fully deserving of the world's sympathy and lots and lots of EU infrastructural grants.

Saying 'What's the story?'

Increasingly this phrase has replaced 'Howaya' as a greeting in Ireland, and is even making inroads in unseating 'Howsitgoinyebigbollixye?' as a popular, affectionate greeting among men. Any non-Irish person should be aware that it is not necessary to take the question literally i.e. one shouldn't start to explain your life story when greeted with 'What's the story?', rather you should respond in kind e.g.

Greeting: 'What's the story?'

Response: 'What's the story?'

There are several variations on the theme, the

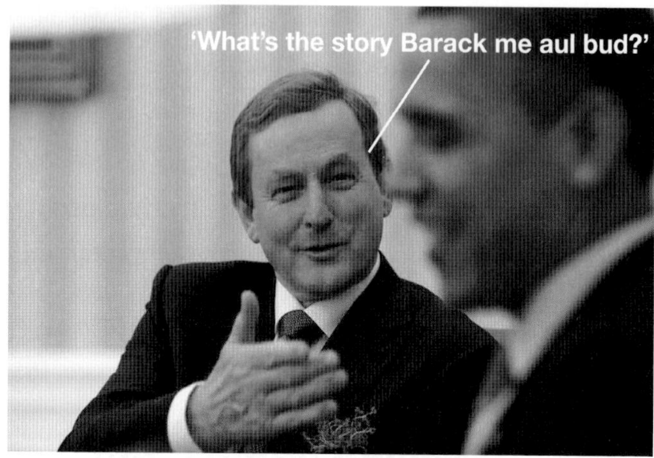

most popular being 'What's the story, bud?' or the pithy 'Story, bud?' or the pithier still 'Story?'

So, for visitors to these shores, do not be unduly disturbed to witness four friends greeting each other thus:

'What's the story, bud?'

'Story?'

'Story with you?'

'Story, bud?'

And then there are those who like to use the Irish version: 'Cad é an scéal?' or simply 'Sceal?' Which leads to conversations like this:

'Cad é an scéal?'

'Scéal with you?'

'Story, bud?'

'What's the scéal?'

And you wondered where Ireland's rich oral tradition came from?

Sin scéal eile, bud.

Uilleann pipes soundtracks.

Whenever a filmmaker wants to tug at Ireland's emotional heartstrings or evoke feelings of nostalgia for days long gone, out come the old uilleann pipe tunes. Whether it's a black & white shot of a bunch of peasants boarding an emigrant ship, a lonely sheep farmer on a mountainside or a Hollywood movie about a heroic rebel Irishman fending off, in slow-motion, an invasion of two-headed aliens from Alpha Centuri, all you have to do is slap on a bit of uilleann pipe music and hey presto, the subject of

the film has suddenly become the embodiment of Ireland's history and character. You want sad? You want happy? Lonely? Pride? Heroism? Passion? Nostalgia? Uilleann pipes are your only man, it seems. Can't you just picture the movie version of the Easter Rising in a few years time? As Padraig Pearse (played by Leonardo DiCaprio) is led out to be executed and the British commander (Daniel Day Lewis) readies the firing squad, up fade the uilleann pipes as we cut away to Pearse's mother weeping alone in her cottage (played by a heavily made-up Angelina Jolie). Ah, it almost brings a tear to your eye just thinking about it. In fact, it might even have you sobbing in despair.

Long pub goodbyes.

Whenever an Irish person in a pub announces that 'I better be off', you can safely assume that what they really mean is 'I better be off in an hour or so.' Behind the apparently sensible decision to go home before we get completely rat-arsed is the deep-felt longing

to stay in the pub and get completely rat-arsed, and be damned with the consequences. This tug-of-war within the Irish psyche has been going on for centuries. Beyond the pub door represents all of life's bad stuff: rain, cold, nagging partner/spouse (usually the wife/girlfriend), mortgage, bills, screaming kids, pressures of work, income taxes, banjaxed country etc. By contrast, within the warm, welcoming embrace of the pub are laughter, friendly chat, gossip, flirting, lightness of mood – in essence all the troubles of the world are unable to penetrate beyond that lovely door. The pub is a refuge, a sanctuary, a bastion impervious to all of life's ills. Which is why it's so bleedin' hard to leave. As a result, most Irish people's departures from their favourite drinking den go something like this:

'Right, I better be off. No, no, I won't (have another one). No, better not. Bye. Goodbye. I'm going. No, I really have to. Look , I'm puttin' on me coat. I am. No, don't order another one. Really don't. I have te go. Good luck. See ye next Friday. No, I really really can't. I need to get off home right now. Oh, alright then, feck it. But just the one, mind. Or a couple. Then I'm off. Really.'

Jim Figgerty.

Admittedly, younger readers may be prompted to say 'Who?' But as anyone Irish over forty can tell you, Jim Figgerty was the man who knew the secret of how they put the figs into the fig rolls. Jim Figgerty is probably Ireland's most famous advertising character and when he first appeared (or rather went missing) in the mid sixties, he quickly became a household name and was much loved the length and breadth of the land. Granted, Ireland's media produced so little in the way of entertainment back then that documentaries about the texture of pig shite in Glocca Morra were also much loved the length and breadth of the land.

The character of Jim Figgerty first appeared as part of a series of teaser press and poster ads, asking the question 'Have you seen this man?' or 'Jim Figgerty please come home'. It was so extensive that many people actually believed Figgerty was a genuine missing person, innocent eejits that we were back then. It was ultimately revealed that Jim Figgerty was the man who knew the secret

recipe, hence the eternally unanswered tagline 'How do Jacobs get the figs into the fig rolls?' which is still used in advertising today.

The campaign expanded into television and a series of ads in which Figgerty was always thwarted just as he was about to reveal the secret. The ads also had an educational value, as Jim, who sometimes had an Arab companion called Habibi, would be asked the question in French: '*Comment Jacobs trouvent-t-ils les figs dans les Fig Rolls*?' (This, incidentally, was the only bit of French we Irish knew until the pop group Labelle came out with 'Lady Marmalade' in 1974, which had the immortal line '*Voulez-vous coucher avec moi (ce soir)?').*

The campaign was created by advertising agency Irish International and lasted for over a decade, during which time there was a race horse named after Figgerty and questions were raised in the Dáil about the character, which only goes to prove that there were as many half-wits in the Dáil back then as there are now.

Anythin' stirrin?

A deadly and relatively recent addition to Ireland's collection of colloquialisms, alongside gems like 'a shower of savages', 'stop de lights' and 'go and ask me arse'. 'Anythin' stirrin?' was first used back in the 1980s by the character Dinny Byrne in the RTÉ series 'Glenroe'. Soon after the two principal characters, Miley and Biddy, are married, Dinny asks his son if there is 'anythin' stirrin'?', or in other words, if he's managed to get Biddy up the spout/in the family way yet. Before the advent of the phrase, you couldn't really come out directly to a woman and ask 'Are you pregnant?' without risking a clatter in the gob. But the personal, nosey nature of the question is disguised by using the witty 'Anythin' stirrin'?' Well, holy God, aren't we just geniuses with de words?

23 A nice bit of buttered turnover.

You can't bate it! This uniquely Irish bread gets its name from the way the dough was folded back on itself, giving it a denser texture and a distinctly odd shape, which occasionally

caused rows in Irish homes as the kids argued with each other as to who got the slice from the big round end, as opposed to the narrow bit that sticks out at the bottom. (Honest te Jaysus, we'd argue about anything in this country.) Dublin's Thomas Street actually used to have bakeries that specialised only in turnovers. The bread's awkward shape made it an absolute bitch to slice without removing sections of your fingers. But the first bite into that buttered thick chunk of fresh turnover was to die for. To hell with yer ciabattas and yer fancy paninis, givvus a nice thick slice of turnover any day!

The Eurovision Song Contest.

Yeah, yeah, you hate the Eurovision. That's what they all say. And that's why about a third of the population admitted to tuning in for the 2011 show, and if you exclude all the little chisellers who were in the land of nod and include all those who didn't admit to watching, probably about ninety percent of the adult population were glued to their sets. So no more of the 'Eurovision is crap' bullshit!

It's quite astonishing that the Eurovision draws such gansey loads of viewers considering that the lyrics of past winners have included such profound gems as 'La la la la la la la la la la la la la la la la la la etc' and such scholastic titles as 'Ding ding a dong' and 'Diggey Loo Diggi Ley'. But who are we to laugh, as, when Dana first won the contest for Ireland back in 1970, she was welcomed home to Ireland with roughly the same level of hoohaa that Neil Armstrong, Buzz Aldrin and Michael Collins were welcomed back from the moon in the U.S.

But if Ireland's Golden Age of Art happened from about AD500-900, our Eurovision Golden Age occurred in the nineties. Johnny Logan's two wins in the 1980s were a mere taste of the wonderful Irish musical treats in store for our European friends, as we scored an unprecedented hat trick between '92 and '94, then had another win in '96. Even in '95, one of Norway's winning duo was Irish. We also had two runners-up in the nineties! Ireland holds virtually every record with regard to the Eurovision: most winners; the only one with three consecutive wins; in the top ten 34 times; highest average points per contest. Like many of the entries, we could go on and on interminably.

We haven't had a win in a long while now (by our standards) and a few years back we even got cocky, sending Dustin the Turkey to represent us as a sort of way of slagging off the whole thing. But many Europeans take their Eurovision very seriously indeed and they didn't get the joke, the dirty shower of savages. In recent years the country has also had to undergo the trauma of *not qualifying*. How dare they? The cheek! What do those European eejits know anyway? To our nation this was akin to Shamrock Rovers telling Lionel Messi that he wasn't good enough to make their first team or The Beatles not getting past the first round of the X Factor. *We are the masters, don't they understand this? We should be granted honorary automatic qualification, for de love of God!*

Our Golden Age of Art may be a part of ancient history. Our Golden Age of Eurovision may be two decades old. But we know, given the depth of our cultural heritage and our great traditions of music and literature that a new Golden Age can't be far away. Because we've got Jedward.

Spittin'

Yep, traditionally we're a nation of spit lovers. At country marts and markets we spit on our hands to seal the deal. It is common practice among many Irish people to spit before shaking hands, which uses the principle of

Farmers in latter day Ireland have taken to donning rubber gloves before sealing the deal

becoming blood brothers without actually having to share bodily fluids internally, but is still a little bit icky. Workmen, in particular, all spit on their palms before lifting a pickaxe or a shovel, in theory to strengthen their grip, but they have continued this practice despite the fact that most wear gloves, presumably because they just like gobbing. In parts of the west of Ireland, it was common for old women to spit on a newborn baby as this was supposed to bring the baby lots of luck, which is ironic as the old hags probably infected countless babies with all sort of ganky diseases. And it's not so long since every cottage and pub came equipped with its own spittoon. These days, surrounded as we are by corrupt bankers, politicians, property developers etc, we can probably expect expectoration to enjoy a huge resurgence in popularity.

26 Saying 'Know what I mean like?'

We use this colloquialism so often you'd begin to wonder if there's something about the way we talk that undermines our confidence that whoever we're talking to won't understand what we're talking about, know what I mean like? Certainly our use of the phrase seems excessive, know what I mean like? For example, why do we consider it necessary to append a simple phrase such as 'I'm going to the shops for a sliced pan' with 'know what I mean like?'

Of course we know what you mean like. Do you think we're stupid? Now there are occasions when the use of 'know what I mean like' might be appropriate, like if the shop assistant was an absolute ride, in which case 'know what I mean like?' would imply that you're not really interested in purchasing a loaf but want to surreptitiously gawk at the assistant's boobs through the Johnston Mooney & O'Brien and Pat the Baker products. But, generally speaking, our endeavours to accentuate our most elementary communications by appending them with a supererogatory question of a frequently rhetorical nature are prodigiously extraneous, know what I mean like?

27 Eating potatoes with every meal.

Okay, it's true that we have expanded our range of tastes beyond the eternal 'maate, sphuds, a bit o' veg and gravy' that was the staple diet of Irish households for generations up to the seventies. Indeed, we have experimented with all sorts of international cuisine, cosmopolitan men and women of the world that we have become. We've tried everything from microwaveable plastic packs of chicken tikka masala to frozen pepperoni pizza, to jars of ready-made chop suey.

But when it comes down to it, slap a plate of bacon, cabbage and spuds in front of an Irish person and they'll still likely declare that 'a good Irish meal bates the shite out of dat oul' foreign muck any day'. Roast beef, parsnips and spuds has the same effect. As does a pork chop, turnips and spuds. You may spot the emergence of a pattern here. The common element in each meal is 'spuds', for the potato seems to be indelibly burnt on to the Irish psyche, much in the same way as enjoying seeing England lose at something.

In his book *The Potato*, American author and historian Larry Zuckerman wrote that 'No European nation has had a longer, more intimate partnership with the potato than Ireland.' Yes, we do love our spuds intimately. We're so in love with the potato that we've adapted its versatile nature to every possible eating occasion. We have fried sliced spuds with breakfast, a pack of Tayto for snack-time, a baked spud for lunch, mashed or boiled spuds for dinner and chips for supper. And why shouldn't we? It is one of the healthiest and most nourishing foods you can eat, (well, except when you chop it up, deep fry it in grease, cover it in salt and then eat it between two slices of buttered sliced pan.) It is so wholesome that entire civilizations and social revolutions have been built on its nourishment, including the mighty Inca Empire, the Hapsburg Empire, the Dutch Empire and the Industrial Revolution. And in Ireland? Well, OK, all we got was Fianna Fáil, but you can't win them all.

Moaning about 'Peig'.

It seemed to generations of us that the educational authorities were determined to ensure we all left school knowing only about ten words of Irish and with a loathing for the language that would endure until our dying day. Besides the wildly hairy, bearded Gaelgoir with the worn out sports jacket that they hired to teach us, and who almost without exception seemed like God's original blueprint for a gobshite, the authorities also inflicted a curriculum on us that was based around a simple premise – 'If ye don't learn your grammar ye'll have the shite beaten out of ye.'

But the final nail in our collective prospects of ever learning to speak Irish was *Peig*. Instead of implanting a vision in our minds of a heroic native Irish speaker battling against a sea of tribulations, poor Peig, the miserable oul' bag, became the woman we loved to loathe. And instead of encouraging us to learn Irish, the language became associated with endless tales of misery, depression and despair, so much so that by the time Irish class had ended, each student felt like they'd been to a funeral on a rainy day in January and then been told their dog had died. Apparently though, the oul' bat wasn't entirely to blame as the state decided that certain parts of her work were unsuitable, so they snipped out the racy bits i.e. they censored the only thing that might just have gripped the attention of hormone-fuelled teenagers. Perhaps they should do a version of *Lady Chatterley's Lover* in Irish – wouldn't it be great to see how they translated all those really naughty words. Perhaps they'd do it the same way they translate things like 'rugby' to 'rugbai' or 'taxi' to 'tacsai'. Just imagine all the fun possibilities! Peig would be turning in her grave.

Deliberately sprinkling our conversation with Irish slang when talking to foreigners.

As referred to in the previous piece about Peig, hardly any of us speak our native language, which means we have to find other ways linguistically to express our national identity. One way we like to do this is to deliberately drop local colloquialisms and slang words into our conversation when engaging with overseas visitors. It's sort of our unofficial native language, which is made up of a few uniquely

Irish words and phrases loosely strung together with a sprinkling of English.

To elaborate a little, imagine a scenario where a couple of Irish guys take their American cousin out for a few pints:

American: 'Say guys, this is a fine bar.'

Mick: 'Yeah, it's deadly when it's not jammers. But sometimes there's a right shower of savages acting the maggot in here, and yer few scoops can be banjaxed.'

American: 'Eh…uh…'

Paddy: 'What Mick means is that in a while there'll be a gansey load of gee-eyed slappers and sleeveens throwin' shapes all over the shop. We should mosey on over to Murphy's if we want a have a bit of craic, know what I mean like?'

American: 'Uh guys…I don't really do drugs.'

Mick & Paddy: 'Ye wha? Sure we just want te go on de batter.'

Fig rolls in custard (see also Jim Figgerty).

This is another of those Irish 'poor man's desserts' from the same stable as the likes of 'ice cream dropped into fizzy orange' that featured in the previous 'Stuff' book. As simple as it sounds,

you just place ten or so fig rolls on a dish and warm them in the oven for five minutes, then cover them in hot custard. Pathetically delicious. Those of you who couldn't even afford fig rolls would substitute bread leftovers smothered in jam. Not something you'd serve to your dinner guests, but still worth the occasional sneaky private indulgence.

For those who couldn't afford jam or custard, it was the sugar sandwiches. Ah, God be with the days. Not.

Ray 'Who put the ball in the English net?' Houghton.

Of all the legendary footballers that Ireland has produced, isn't it gas that arguably the most loved of them all is good old Ray. Was he the most talented of the lot? Probably not, although he was certainly talented. Was he our record goalscorer? Not by a mile! He scored six goals as opposed to the current record of fifty-three by Robbie Keane. Is it because he is such a wonderful, warm-hearted and charming personality? He's undoubtedly a nice guy, but no, we don't all want to marry him. No, we love him principally because of a single moment in his long and distinguished career, when Ray put the ball in the English net at Euro '88.

Yes, it was as though we'd gotten them back for our '700 years of oppression' in the blink of an eye! We'd just retrospectively defeated marauding armies of Elizabeth I and Cromwell. A million dead in the Famine? Here's the payback. 1916 Rising? Payback. Black & Tans? Take that, ye murderous bowsies!

Dismissed as no-hopers by the English media, Ray's goal clamped millions of gobs shut in England and led to riotous celebrations by Irish men, women and children around the globe. Six years later, Ray put a cherry on the top by scoring another solitary winning goal against the arrogant Italians in Giants Stadium, New York. If we loved him before, we adored, adulated and worshipped him now. To paraphrase Bill Shankly, Ray's goal against England was not a matter of life and death, it was much more important than that.

32 References to Ireland in movies or on television.

It's funny the way a fleeting reference to Ireland or Irish people in a Hollywood movie or an Australian soap opera stirs a bit of pride in us. We almost treat it as though we'd unexpectedly heard our name on the radio – Hey! That's me they're talking about! Whether it's a question of featuring thousands of Irish extras doing battle in kilts in 'Braveheart' or a passing remark about some obscure American character being 'Irish', we can't help but have a sneaking admiration for ourselves.

How often do you hear references to things Belgian or Danish or German, huh? Hardly ever! But Ireland? Every second movie or TV show has an Irish character, location, actor, focus puller or 2nd assistant boom operator. These little things serve to remind us of the fact that we enjoy a hugely disproportionate influence on the world, and that we've made such a bollox of our country that most of our brightest talents have to emigrate to get a job.

Having loads of literary geniuses.

We may be absolutely wojus at producing lots of quality politicians, bankers, planners, county councillors etc, but in the area of writing, to employ a suitably literary description, we're bleedin' rapid. We've been churning out geniuses for centuries: Oliver Goldsmith, Oscar Wilde, James Joyce, Bram Stoker, Brendan Behan, George Bernard Shaw, Richard Brinsley Sheridan, Samuel Beckett, Seamus Heaney... one could go on almost indefinitely. The great pride we take in our rich literary heritage is reflected in the fact that ninety per cent of us have never read a single word that they wrote, except of course the stuff that we had battered into us in school. Most Irish people would be hard pressed to name a single title of a book, play or poem created by many of the above. But we do love them all the

Oscar Wilde Statue at Merrion Square

same, principally for the fame and prestige they have brought to our little country. We're sort of like those characters that hang around pop or movie stars in the hope that some of the fame and glamour will rub off. Yet for a tiny country continually to generate giants of literature by the gansey-load just proves how superior we really are to everyone else on the planet.

34 A nice bit of buttered Barmbrack.

As Irish as Padraig Pearse's shillelagh, barmbrack was traditionally served at Halloween and usually had a ring, a coin or other token hidden inside it. Old custom had it that the token you happened to get in your slice was a sign of things to come in the year ahead. So, if you got a ring you'd end up hitched, a coin and you'd come into some

money, a bullet and you'd be rightly fucked.

Another custom was to smother the slice of barmbrack in butter, which further helped to conceal the token and greatly increased the chances of someone choking to death on a thruppeny bit, thereby denying them the chance to be rich.

Barmbrack is essentially sweet bread mixed with fruit that has been soaked in tea. The word reputedly comes from the Irish *báirín* meaning loaf and *breac* meaning trout, so it is essentially fish cake. Seriously though, as a trout is speckled, the word *breac* also translates as such, so we're left with 'speckled loaf'. Irish barmbrack is usually served with tea and accompanied by comments like ''Tis very nice, ah but it's not as good as me Mammy's'.

35 Saying 'Naaa' instead of 'no'.

The great thing about 'Irish English' is that it's so much more expressive than English itself. Here's the perfect example. In English 'no' means 'no' – there's essentially no room for misinterpretation. But as we Irish rarely like to commit ourselves absolutely to a particular course of action, we've invented the word 'naaa' as an alternative, which allows us to sort of say 'no', but leaves open the possibility of changing our minds somewhere down the line or denying we'd said 'no' in the first place. 'Naaa' in reality means 'I'm thinking about it'. Let's return to our favourite place, the pub, to demonstrate.

'Fancy a pint, Seamus?'

'Naaa.'

'Sure?'

'Alright then.'

Quod erat demonstrandum, as they might say in Ballydehob.

Pretending we're still Catholics.

Despite our often vociferous protestations to the contrary, we take a certain pride in being Catholics in Ireland, notwithstanding the fact that the next time most of us visit a church we'll be horizontal and in a wooden box.

Anecdotally, it seems that about ninety percent of the country are avowed atheists, yet recent census returns suggest that about eighty-five percent still define ourselves as Catholics. It's another of those strange Irish contradictions, the result of our unique ability to hold two entirely opposing viewpoints at the same time, such as the gobshites a few years back who were wearing Manchester United shirts while protesting in Croke Park about its use for 'foreign games'. Even if a large proportion of us still do retain a certain level of belief in things spiritual, many don't bother to practise what they preach, especially since the downfall of the 'Big Brother' version of the Catholic Church. This new religion is much more flexible, especially as it allows us to have loads of dirty thoughts and indulge in all sorts of kinky shenanigans without the merest hint of guilt. And best of all, you don't have to go to Mass on Sunday!

Even so, most of us still call ourselves Catholic and the reasons for this have almost nothing to do with religion, but are related to our other great devotion – not being feckin' British. Religion in Ireland became inextricably entwined with nationalism as far back as the Cromwellian invasion and we've had plenty of time to cement the bonds of Catholicism and patriotism since then. So we dutifully fill in 'Catholic' in the census form, as to put anything else would be like putting 'Not fully Irish' in the nationality box.

It is best summed up by an old joke north and south of the border about a guy who wanders into an area of Belfast controlled by paramilitaries. When stopped, he is asked which foot he kicks with, ie what's his religion.

'I'm an atheist,' he replies.

'Yeah, pal, but are you a Catholic atheist or a Protestant atheist?'

Deliberately pronouncing phrases with a thick country accent.

This is not just the preserve of the Dubs but is also common among Ireland's rural population, all of whom love to adopt a wojusly thick culchie accent on occasion, either to emphasize or perhaps take the mick out of something. In order to accomplish this, certain rules have to be applied, and a few of the principal ones are listed below, along with some examples, allowing you to practise or fine tune this particular skill.

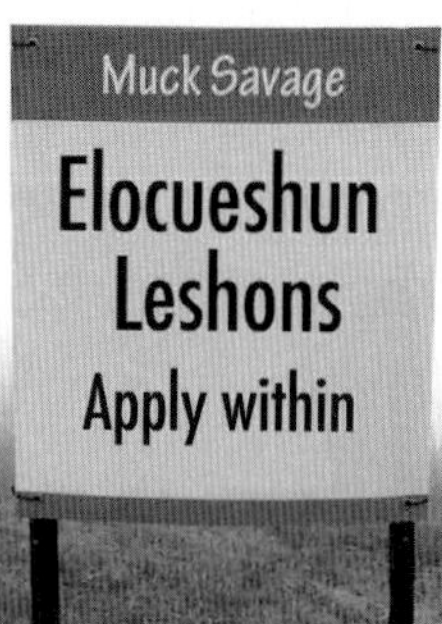

Drop the 'g' in all 'ing' word endings.

Never use 'you', 'your' or 'you're'. 'Ye' or 'yer' are acceptable replacements.

Replace 'ee' or 'ie' with 'ay'.

Any word starting with 'sl' becomes 'shl'.

The letter 'm' in a word should always be preceded by an 'e'.

Combine any two words when one ends in a consonant and the next starts with a vowel.

'To' is always replaced with 'te'.

Always drop the 'f' in 'of'.

They're the basics, although the grammatical rules for speaking 'extreme mucksavage' are too innumerable and complex to reproduce here. Let's look at some examples:

'I'm off te Shligo for a few schoops and den I'm off te shleep.'

'Now yer suckin' daysel.'

'She's a fine bit o' sthuff but she'd get up on a sthiff wind.'

'I'd an unmerciful fayed o' shteak an' sphuds.'

'He wouldn't work te warem himself'.

'G'wan te feck outtedat.'

Moaning about stuff to Joe Duffy.

The answer to all our ills is Joe Duffy, the nation's sympathetic ear, our sounding board, the septic tank into which we excrete all of our woes. He is Ireland's big Mammy to whom you can recount all of your troubles, and you know how Irish people love running to their mammies when the slightest little ill befalls them.

No problem is too big or small to warrant a call to Joe. Been offended by a 'swearword' you heard in a song? Ring Joe Duffy and maybe he'll launch a nationwide campaign to get it banned. Think Irish criminals have it too cushy in jail? Joe'll sort those bowsies out. Want a head-shop closed? Consider it out of business. Been ripped off for fifty euro by a plumber? The whole nation wants to hear about it. Had to wait an hour for a bus? Millions are agog at the prospect of listening

to your tragic tale. Got a wart on your arse? Joe Duffy. Erectile dysfunction? Joe Duffy. One boob implant bigger than the other? Joe Duffy. Think RTÉ radio presenters are paid obscenely excessive salaries in times of deep recession and spiralling unemployment? Whatever you do, don't ring Joe Duffy.

Jam sambos.

Many older readers may recall that while attending primary school in Ireland there was a daily ritual of queuing up for a state-provided snack at break time. And as the state was constantly on the verge of bankruptcy, this consisted of a tiny bottle of milk and a slice of bread covered in a thin layer of margarine, which frequently prompted the use of quaint child-hood sayings such as 'I hate this ganky shite', and when consumed produced an expression on most kids' faces akin to a bulldog licking piss off a nettle. But just one day a week the kids were in for a treat, when the manky margarine was replaced with strawberry jam. This brought exhortations of such joy and relief from the children you'd think they'd been granted an entire month homework-free. The jam sambos were so loved that trades were offered for Dinky cars and Hotspur comics.

The jam sambo was a staple of the Irish diet then. It could be consumed as lunch, as a snack, as a dessert or a supper and it had the great benefit of being as cheap as a slapper's make-up. It sort of vanished in recent times thanks to the Celtic Tiger, as many people would have been a bit ashamed to admit they didn't have a villa in Spain so they certainly weren't going to admit to a liking for jam sambos. But now, in recessionary times, it's making a big comeback and the only argument is whether a jam sambo tastes better with buttered bread or plain bread.

You're thinking of having one right now, aren't you? Go on, nobody else need know about it. Put down the book, sneak into the kitchen and start slapping that raspberry or blackcurrant or strawberry jam onto the ol' sliced pan! And make a nice sup o' tae while you're there. Now, sink your teeth into that. Ah, heaven.

Saying 'Stop the lights'.

One of those phrases that is uniquely Irish and one that has been passed down through the generations, although younger folk will probably be startled, horrified or disbelieving of the TV show from which it originated. The expression itself, for non-Irish readers, means 'Hang on!' or 'Hold everything!' and began its life in possibly the worst TV quiz show in the history of international broadcasting. It was called 'Quicksilver', hosted by a man called

Bunny Carr, and ran from the mid-sixties until the end of the seventies. Featuring a row of illuminated numbers, the unvetted contestants had to answer a question, and the longer he or she took, the more

lights went out, reducing the 'prize money' on offer. If you were struggling to answer a particularly tricky question such as 'How many sides has a square?' or 'How do you spell your name, Mary?' you could stall the lights by yelling 'Stop the lights!'

The generation who have been reared on such shows as the 'Million Pound Drop' and 'Who wants to be a Millionaire?' should now either sit down or hold onto something to prevent them from fainting, as we're about to reveal the 'prizes' on offer. Answering the first question won you the grand sum of 1d, that's one old penny. Now, admittedly, inflation has considerably reduced the value of 1d in today's monetary terms, but it is safe to say that even back in the sixties 1d would barely buy you a discarded toe nail clipping. But it got better. Because the next question held a reward of three pence. And so on and so forth, until at the end of the day, if you were some sort of fountain of knowledge and a walking encyclopaedia who knew the answer to everything in the universe, the reward for your genius might be about fifty or sixty pounds. Not that anyone ever left the studio with such wealth. Usually you might win enough bus fare to get you as far as Ballyfermot, which was unfortunate, as you probably lived in Portlaoise.

But the best bit was the answers to some of the questions, which have become a treasured part of Irish folklore.

Q: (Pic of native American Indian) 'Which country is this person from?'

A: 'India.'

Q: 'What is the Ayatollah?'

A: 'A céilidh band.' (The Tulla céilidh band was popular at the time)

Q: 'Which Kildare town sounds like a part of the body?' (Athy)

A: 'Kilcock.'

Q: 'What was Hitler's first name?'

A: 'Heil.'

Wearing giant leprechaun hats at Irish sports events.

You'd like to think that there's an element of self-deprecation in Irish sports fans wearing giant green leprechaun top hats at international matches, soccer in particular, and that we're taking the piss out of the clichéd image of Ireland that we've had to endure for so long. Please God, let's hope that's the reason men and women alike love wearing these hats, and that those who wear them are trying to be witty, as opposed to half-witty.

Also, you really don't want to end up sitting directly behind one of these eejits at a game, affording you a view only of a mass of green polyester and a 'Made in China' tag.

It may also come as a shock to the leprechaun hat brigade, that if they really want to look like a leprechaun they should be wearing a green bowler hat, not a top hat, so not only do they look like gobshites, but they've no sense of leprechaun style either.

On the plus side, these ginormous bits of tack do have one practical use as it seems many fans have been using them to subvert a certain airline's rigid rules on the amount of baggage that you're allowed carry onto the plane. Apparently you can cram as much as five kilograms of material up there.

Michael Collins outwitting the English (not to mention shooting them).

With all the lousy defeats we suffered at the hands of the English down the centuries (*see* 'Our 700 years of oppression'), it's great that we have one hero to cling to who managed to turn the tables against overwhelming odds and kick some English arse! (Apologies to our English friends, but you kicked ours so often, well, can you blame us?) But it's not just the fact that he staged countless guerrilla attacks and blew loads of the gougers back to Blighty, it's the fact that he was so smart he made them look like an experiment in artificial stupidity. They had their entire army and police network scouring the country for him for years and he just waltzed or cycled by them as cocky as you like dressed as a priest or, on occasions, a woman. For Jaysus' sake, he even managed to break into Dublin Castle, the seat of their 'intelligence'. It's nice to think of him sniggering to himself as he passed through checkpoint after checkpoint and then whispering, 'what a bunch of gobshites!'

Brown envelopes.

Sadly, the Ireland that Michael Collins and others fought and died for was largely hijacked by a bunch of gougers whose chief obsession was not the betterment of the nation but with the acquisition of 'brown envelopes.' These harmless bits of folded paper have become synonymous with political life in Ireland, much the same way that diarrhoea is synonymous with irritable bowel syndrome. Ireland is surely the only place in the world where uttering the word 'envelope' in a Presidential debate will provoke howls of derisory laughter from the audience. Once upon a time, the brown envelope was associated with things like letters from the taxman or the dreaded arrival of your school report. But what innocent days those were in retrospect.

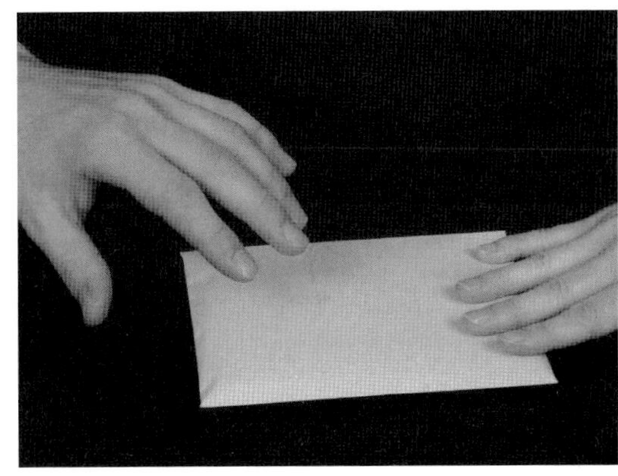

For decades now, if you wanted anything done in terms of, say, planning approval or getting a licence to run a particular business, first thing you did was to head off to your nearest Eason's and purchase a pack of brown envelopes, which you would fill with wads of cash to slip to some cute hoor councillor, and hey presto, you've got permission to build three hundred houses in a flood plain three kilometres from a road. Who gave a shite? But it wasn't only mere county councillors whose pockets were stuffed with bulging brown envelopes. Nope. All the way to the summit of Irish political life, Ireland danced to the sound of rustling brown envelopes. No office was worthy of respect. Ministerial offices were merely repositories of more and more brown envelopes.

But what about the country? What about the people?

As they say in Drumcondra, 'F-f-fuck the p-p-people. Where's me f-f-feckin' envelope?'

Saying 'Shite' as opposed to 'shit'.

Shit is for wimps, an effete Americanism that as a swear word is as effective and useless as tits on a bull. Now, if you really want to express your anger or to comment on the quality of something, 'shite' is your only man. 'Shite' is a real man's swear word, carrying that extra cutting edge, truly reflecting your emotional state. On top of that, 'shite' has a heritage that reaches back centuries into Irish history, whereas 'shit' only

came to prominence through Hollywood films in recent decades. In the eighteenth century, for example, a favourite practice of ours was to 'kick the shite out of foreign landlords', and when the leaders of the 1916 Rising saw all the Brits massing down below in O'Connell Street, they shouted a collective 'Oh shite!'. Yes, 'shite' has true cultural significance. So remember, in the great lexicon of swear words, our 'shite' beats their 'shit' hands down any day.

Sending out bits of wedding cake to people who hadn't made the wedding.

This used to be common practice until recently and is still done by some. Only those who had sent a wedding present would be a beneficiary of a

tiny slice of cake, which would arrive in a cute little specially designed box. Unfortunately, by the time it had been through the hands of twenty burly sorting office head-the-balls in An Post, then crammed through your letterbox, it would emerge as a brown, squashed lump of fetid gunge. Often, only the icing would survive intact, as in those days it was made to be bullet-proof.

If you were lucky enough to get one of these little 'treats', the usual course of action was to destroy it immediately with a blow-torch to prevent the spread of disease. But in days of yore, unmarried girls in the house would often secrete the cake under their pillow in the belief that they would dream of the man they would one day marry.

Usually all that happened, though, was that they would wake from some horrible nightmare in which they'd been attacked by a giant lump of battered wedding cake.

Putting a few bob on the horses.

Among our favourite vices, alongside drink, swearing, begrudgery and accepting bribes, having a 'flutter' on the nags accounts for about four billion euro a year, and that's one bejaysus of a flutter. That's roughly equivalent to about half the money the government spends on education each year, or about the same amount it pays in bonuses to incompetent bank officials.

Gambling on the horses has been given a certain respectability by the fact that 'the sport of kings' has a tradition going back millennia in Ireland, and while we haven't had any kings for about four hundred years, we're obviously happy to spend a king's ransom betting on it on a daily basis.

Stroll past a betting shop any day and you can

observe grown men (mostly, though not exclusively) poring over the racing pages with the same intensity as a revenue inspector studying your tax return. The hopeful punter will then place a little bet on a seven-to-one nag called something daft like 'Cuchulainn's Hurley' or 'Luminous Y-Fronts'.

Often this 'little bet' will bear a striking resemblance in terms of size to this month's mortgage or the weekly household budget. Watch as, fifteen minutes later, the individual emerges, wearing the same expression as a man who's been fired and whose dog has died and whose wife has just told him she's having an affair with his best friend.

Naturally, the aficionados will tell you that's it's not about the winning, it's about the thrill you experience before you lose all your money, along with your house, wife and kids.

But on a lighter and related note, there is a story, perhaps apocryphal, but who cares, that in the sixties when most gamblers listened to their horse racing on the radio, an Irish trainer decided to have a little joke on the then censorious RTÉ by entering a horse called *The Country Member* in a race. Nothing remarkable about that, you'd think, until the following Saturday afternoon when oul' lads in pubs and oul' dears in their kitchens listened with gaping mouths to the commentary that was being beamed all over the nation...

...and just coming into the final straight is The Cunt Remember! It's The Cunt Remember by two lengths! He's pulling away! The Cunt Remember is the winner by almost three lengths...a fantastic ride by The Cunt Remember!

Blaming a 'bad pint'.

The single greatest source of illness in Ireland. It is known to cause

severe headaches, nausea, diarrhoea, vomiting, stomach and muscular cramps and erectile dysfunction. The 'bad pint' has resulted in more lost work days than an outbreak of bubonic plague. There have been so many bad pints served in Ireland you'd wonder if our great brewers throw dead rats into the vats of fermenting ale just for a bit of craic. Luckily, there is help at hand, as the bad pint can often be identified before consumption.

Usually the 'bad pint' is the one you've had after your tenth or eleventh pint or the one you're about to consume immediately after you've imbibed your own body weight in beer. Another indicator of a 'bad pint' is that there may appear to be two 'bad pints' before your eyes, or if the pint you're about to consume appears to 'wobble', as though you're seeing it through a heat haze.

These are indicators that your previous pint might also not have been up to scratch and that your vision is already being affected. Lastly 'bad pints' can be identified by the fact that they are usually accompanied by an apparently disembodied voice saying something like, 'Gooowaaan Shayyymush, won lasssst won forrrr de roaaad.'

Italian chippers.

Ah yes, the wonderful, masterful cuisine of Italia: Crespelle alla Fiorentina, Ossobuco alla Milanese, Arrosto all'Arancio… so, naturally, when those artisans of Italian food arrived in Ireland all those years ago, they studied the level of sophistication of the Irish palate and then decided to devote all their culinary skills to making chips. And, thank God they did, otherwise the effects of the bad pint mentioned in the previous section would have been so much the worse without the soakage those precious chips provided.

But how on earth did Italians end up associated with making chips in Ireland? Legend has it that one Giuseppe Cervi was on his way to America in 1880 when the ship docked at Cobh. He got off for a stroll around and ended up strolling all the way to Dublin. There he started off by selling roast chestnuts but the story goes that one day he accidentally roasted a piece of potato and a customer complimented it. Luckily for all the millions of plastered Irish people since, Giuseppe decided that the Irish knew a tasty spud when they ate one and was soon running a shop in Pearse Street selling deep fried chips and fish. His wife spoke little English and would point to the menu, saying, '*Uno di questo, uno di quello?*' which translates as 'One of these, one of those?' eventually evolving into the pithier 'one and one', which is much easier to say when you've had ten vodka and reds.

Word of Giuseppe's success spread back to an area in his homeland called Casalattico in Val Di Comino, which is between Rome and Naples, and before you know it we were being invaded by the Macaris, Caffollas, the Fuscos, the Borzas and the Caffellos. And how we embraced them. Because, for many Irish people, sophisticates that we are, the culinary highlight of our week is a battered ray and chips smothered in salt and vinegar and consumed in a bus shelter at 1am. Oh, and don't forget the battered onion rings, Luigi. And *grazie mille*!

The Fields of Athenry.

Like 'Olé Olé Olé', 'The Fields of Athenry' has long been a favourite of Irish football supporters and subsequently Celtic football supporters and then Liverpool supporters. Irish international rugby fans were next to take up the chant, followed by Munster and Leinster rugby supporters, followed by boxing fans, hockey fans, racing fans, hurling fans and every other fan of every godforsaken sport in the country. Because of its sad tale about a man being exiled to Botany Bay during the Famine for having stolen Trevelyan's corn, many people assume the song dates from that era, but it was actually written in the 1970s by Irishman Pete St. John who also penned that other 'ancient' song 'The Rare Ould Times'. Nevertheless its tale of British oppression and injustice naturally stirs our passion for revenge and for wreaking

bloody violence on our opponents. The hero of the story, Michael, is chained up in a ship and sent packing to Australia, so, in effect, it is a tale of sadness, despair and defeat, which is also appropriate for most Irish sports teams.

The state of yerwan.

Such is the frequency with which we employ this colloquialism that

many overseas visitors mistakenly believe that we have a fascination with some little-known middle-eastern or African tin pot country called 'The State of Yerwan'. Little do they realise that this is our favourite way to refer disparagingly to any girl who, in the opinion of the speaker, is making a right eejit of herself, or has dressed inappropriately. Spoken with equal enthusiasm by men and women, it is normally reserved for girls who are walking around with a skirt halfway up their arse and with their boobs attempting to burst through the miniscule and flimsy piece of pink textile that is just barely attached to their chest.

Alternatively, it may be employed when a girl has slightly overindulged in alcohol and is staggering around bumping into people, chairs, lampposts and moving vehicles, and puking at the same time.

'The state of yerwan' is also a useful tool for other girls who just want to be bitchy and may employ it to slag off a particular dress another girl is wearing or her hairdo, and it is especially handy when one girl spots another flirting with someone she fancies herself, in which case it is uttered with complete disgust.

There is a male equivalent in 'The state of yerman', but somehow it doesn't have the same ring to it. Perhaps because that's the sort of thing you'd expect from 'yerman' but being a girl, 'yerwan' should know better. It's one of the mysteries of the rich, complex tapestry of our spoken language.

Being self-deprecating.

Besides slagging each other, another of our beloved pastimes is slagging ourselves. Some examples:

'I'm so fat me arse size is méasured in acres.'

'I know so little about technology I thought you bought a Bluetooth at the dentist.'

'I'm so ugly that when I was born the doctor slapped me mother.'

This modesty is a wonderful national trait and adds considerably to the humour of our conversation.

Or is it?

Well, according to the most recent issue of *Lonely Planet*, our 'garrulous sociability and self-deprecating twaddle' hides a 'dark secret' – that we are low on self-esteem. The Irish are therefore 'suspicious of praise and don't believe anything nice ever said about them.'

Yeah, well, to the writers of *Lonely Planet* we should explain that, besides self-deprecating humour, we also do deprecating humour very well, much of which was likely uttered the moment you left the room. Here are a few examples of what was probably said about you:

'It's hard to see that guy's point of view, as most people can't see that far up their own arse.'

'That gobshite would wring drink out of a floozie's knickers.'

'Yerwan was as sharp as a hurley.'

'I'd say yer man is the sap in the family tree.'

'That wagon had a face like the back of a turf cart.'

You see, the other thing is that while we do love slagging each other, nobody else is allowed to slag us, ye gobshites! Put that in your next bleedin' edition.

Being European.

Although the Irish love affair with Europe has been going through a bit of a rocky patch of late, it's quite likely that in the end we'll kiss and make up and even end up fully sharing the European bed and screwing them for everything we can get. You see, we've always been attracted to the notion of being European. We like the ring of it. They have cool stylish stuff in Europe, like Lamborghinis, cannelloni, Coco Chanel, topless beaches, Gaudi and schnapps, whereas we have spice burgers, Dunnes Stores, fat arses, stout and Liberty Hall.

Besides the image, the other great thing about being European was all the spondulicks they used to give us during the first couple of decades of our membership of the EU. You'd be driving along a nice, shiny new bit of motorway and there'd be signs all over the place reading something like: 'This project was part funded by the European Infrastructural Fund'. What 'part funded' actually meant was that if the motorway cost two hundred million euro, then the EU paid one hundred and ninety-nine million, nine hundred and ninety-nine

thousand, nine hundred and ninety euro, and we paid the other tenner.

But more than all of that, it is not so much that we like the notion of being 'European' as that we absolutely adore the notion of being 'not-British'. By associating ourselves with the Pierres and the Gunthers and the Marios of this world, we are distancing ourselves from the 'Arrys and the Alfies and from our British-dominated past.

The European mainland is a humungous big wedge we can use to separate ourselves from the 'ould enemy'. If we could afford it we'd build a big bridge from Rosslare that skirts Land's End and hooks up with Europe just north of Paris. We're not so much a member of the EU as of the WANBU: The We Are Not British Union.

So, Europe, are you listening? We've demonstrated by a multiplicity of reasons our unswerving loyalty and commitment to the European ideal.

Now, can we have some more free cash, please?

53 A nation holds its breath.

Our favourite sporting moment of all time. RTÉ sports commentator George Hamilton delivered the now-immortal line as David O'Leary stepped up to take the final penalty against Romania in Italia '90. A moment later approximately one million pints of beer were spilled, Irish men hugged other Irish men, women who up to then thought a striker was a guy with a placard, cried openly. Strangers snogged, enemies embraced, Mammies fainted, dogs hid in terror and Charlie Haughey tried to make some political capital.

In our collective memories it was the moment that ended the depression and gloom of the eighties and heralded in a new era of eh...well, let's not go there. Best to recall the moment as most Irish people who weren't lucky enough to be at the match do: the TV screen, the goal, the Guinness flying through the air, the TV screen moving from your field of vision as another human being rugby tackles you in a show of emotion, your face pressed against the pub carpet, the feel of the soggy polyester as a girl's stiletto heel pierces your cheek. Ah what joy!

54 Saying 'God forgive ye'.

You remark in passing that Mr O'Neill who runs the local grocery store is a right bleedin' gouger who just overcharged you by fifty cents for a Mars bar, and your mammy responds with an indignant 'God forgive ye!' She will then go on to rebuke you for speaking ill of the man and for using a mild profanity, all the while thinking that the oul' bastard O'Neill has been ripping people off for years and should be strung up by the goolies.

Daughter remarks to mother while attending family function that her cousin Fiona is a right slapper. Response? 'God forgive ye!' While the very thought that one of her blood relations could be such a creature makes her cringe, she has to admit that the total amount of cloth in Fiona's outfit would barely make a handkerchief and she does harbour dark suspicions that Fiona has shagged the entire local hurling team. Still, she feels compelled to plead for the Almighty's forgiveness for such a slight.

While the phrase has sort of gone out of general fashion, it is still much beloved of our mammies, who frequently use it to express false outrage as in the examples above.

And if your mammy sees you reading this filth? 'God forgive ye!'

55 Loving bankers and then hating bankers.

A few short years ago we were falling over ourselves to tell everyone what a kind and understanding person our local bank manager was. The bank manager was a hero of Ireland, a veritable Brian Boru of the lending world, doing battle against want; a Mother Teresa of banking who gave freely to the needy; a Sigmund Freud of finance who listened to your problems and analysed them, then took all your worries away with the simple words, 'How much d'ye want?'

Nothing was beyond his kindness. No folly of yours, however ridiculous, would be met with anything other than a smile, a nod of understanding and a handshake. Want to buy a sixteen-bedroom villa in Tahiti on a salary of thirty thousand a year? Sign here. Need an all-terrain Antarctic 7-litre SUV to drive to work at the hairdressers? No problem. Want to hire a doorman to admit your visitors to your three bed semi-detached in Ballygobackwards? Great idea!

What a lovely man or woman your bank manager was. How we collectively loved him.

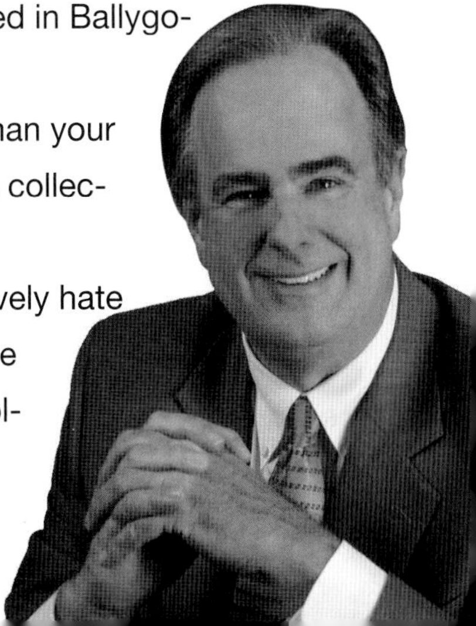

And now, how we collectively hate his or her guts. How naive we were: like an innocent schoolgirl we believed all our seducer told us, not realising that we were being lined up to be shagged from here to kingdom come and back again. The bastards almost threw the money at us, and like the greedy gobshites we were, we grabbed it. Of course our friendly bankers never told us that our purchases would be worthless in a couple of years, but they'd still want their pound of flesh every month. The smiles and handshakes and nods were suddenly gone, replaced by scowls and threats.

In a few short months we went from 'What a lovely chap' to 'I'd love to give that smug, overpaid scumbag a root up the arse!' What a fickle nation we are!

Cricket (briefly).

For a few brief hours in 2011, all of Ireland fell in love with cricket.

The very notion of this a few years beforehand would have had us all guffawing heartily the length and breadth of Ireland, or to put it in more colloquial terms, breaking our shite laughing. Cricket?

That pansy's game? Real men don't play cricket. That's for wimpy English chaps from places like Eton and Cambridge, who say things like, 'I say, ruddy fine strike, Carruthers. Bravo, dear boy! Bravo!'

'For Jaysus' sake', we used to say, 'imagine dressing up in all white! What are they – Girls? Then they run up and down a short bit of grass and chuck a ball at each other for ten minutes before stopping for cups of tea and dainty little pink biscuits. First sign of a drop of rain and they suspend play. What sort of big girls' blouses are they? Put them in a hurling match and they wouldn't last five…etc etc'

Yep, that was our general view of cricket up until recently.

Then, a few years back, the Irish cricket team suddenly appeared on our radar by beating the fourth-ranked team in the world, Pakistan, precipitating a national outpouring of shock and grief in that country. Suddenly we sat up and cocked an eye in the direction of these green-clad Irish cricketers in the far-off West Indies. For most people it was a revelation that we even had a cricket team.

But after that brief flirtation we sort of forgot about it for a few years, distracted as we were by our country disappearing down the jacks. Then along comes the next World Cup and naturally most Irish people hadn't a clue it was happening. But then, on 2 March 2011, word started to filter through from India that something startling was happening in the world of cricket. In barber shops, offices, cars, kitchens, pubs, factories all over the country, Irish ears began to prick up. Ireland was on the verge of pulling off possibly the biggest upset in cricket history by beating, (oh it doesn't get any better than this), England! To express it in terms of a different sport, this was the equivalent of England beating us at hurling, or the Tubbercurry Ladies Camogie team beating the Japanese at Sumo Wrestling. Not only that, but Ireland's Kevin O'Brien hit the fastest ever World Cup century and prompted the Taoiseach to comment: 'Their supreme effort will lift the spirits of every single Irish person, no matter where they are in the world.' Now we never thought we'd hear that in the context of cricket!

Cricket terms were suddenly being bandied about in pubs. Finally we understood that an 'all rounder' was not a very fat person, a 'paddle scoop' was not for picking up your dog's turds, 'LBW' was not the 36th President of the USA and 'caught behind' was not when a guy grabbed a girl's arse. How we loved cricket, for that brief moment the greatest game on earth.

Then again if we happen to beat England in the world Elephant Polo championships, we'll love that too. Or Basque pelota. Or underwater rugby. Or egg rolling. Or...

Sally O'Brien.

Who the hell's Sally O'Brien, many of you under-thirties may ask. The lovely Sally was a 'character' in an ad for Harp, way back in the 1980s who won the hearts of all the men of Ireland with her sultry, sexy, teasing, come-get-me eyes while the voiceover of the far-

away emigrant reminisced: '...and Sally O'Brien, and the way she might look at you'. It is a sad reflection on the state of the place at the time that this was the nearest many Irish men came to sex. It turned out that Sally O'Brien was actually English, the actress Vicky Michelle, more familiar to TV audiences at the time as the sexy wartime French waitress in the comedy series ''Allo 'Allo'. French, English or Irish, the fictional Sally fuelled the fantasies of many a sad fecker. Maybe with the new generation of emigrants they might consider bringing her back. 'And the way that oul' wan Sally O'Brien might look at ye…'

58 Our very clever megalithic ancestors.

More evidence that we sprang from the most advanced, most intelligent race on earth. OK the pyramids may be a *bit* bigger, but Newgrange, Knowth, Dowth etc are a thousand years older and much more clever. Ha! And they're at least five hundred years older than Stonehenge. We'd figured out the path of the sun when the Brits were still swinging through the trees, chanting 'Uhh uhh uhh', much like any Saturday night in Bristol nowadays. And the Romans? That shower of savages were crouching in caves beside the Tiber when we were tossing up gigantic dolmens by the dozen.

Then, somewhere along the line it all stopped, and instead of evolving into one of the greatest civilisations on the planet, we ended up with a bunch of cute hoors. Either there was a strike for better working conditions or they ran out of cement or something. Still, the seed of greatness was obviously there, and still is. For example, you can still observe similarities between modern Ireland and megalithic society. A dolmen like the gigantic one at Browneshill in Carlow weighed one hundred tons and would have required a thousand men working for months on end to complete the job. Similarly today, having a one hundred metre stretch of a country lane resurfaced, also requires thousands of men working for months on end.

Wanderly Wagon.

Growing up in Ireland in the sixties and seventies usually prompts memories such as being threatened with the eternal fires of hell if you so much as uttered a swear word like 'bleedin', or living in mortal fear of your teacher in case you got one of your long division sums wrong. One of the few diversions for Irish children from the nightmarish thought of their flesh roasting for eternity was to spend a relaxing thirty minutes in front of their old TV set watching the adventures of the colourful Wanderly Wagon.

Actually, the efforts of the set decorators at the time were a bit of a waste of time as the audience was watching on black & white televisions. Kids from three to twelve sat there transfixed as, in a startling display of technologically advanced special effects, the jittery wagon would take off over a papier mache landscape and hurtle across the sky with the grace of a drunken pigeon. But, to be kind, the characters of O'Brien, Judge, Godmother, Crow, Rory etc were much loved, and among the renowned writers can be numbered Oscar-winning director Neil Jordan and actor Frank Kelly [later Father Jack Hackett in 'Father Ted'.] A poll about people's favourite character conducted on the website boards.ie (yes, people conduct polls on such things) found that the friendly and wise long-eared dog, Judge, was the most loved. The evil, plotting, greedy, conspiring, Sneaky Snake was the least favourite puppet character, which is surprising as we subsequently made him Taoiseach three times in a row.

60 Deliberately wearing your county colours into your greatest rival's county.

A very popular way of proclaiming your loyalty to your county, and, more to the point, of rubbing your nearest county's nose in the cowshite if you've recently beaten them. Actually, while this is immensely popular in Ireland, the best aspect of it is that it rarely results in bloody carnage despite the intense rivalries that often exist between neighbouring counties.

Reports of someone getting the shite kicked out of them because they were wearing a particular county's colours are incredibly rare.

You try doing something similar in Glasgow and see how far you'll get. A Celtic-clad fan wandering into a Rangers area, or vice versa, will be identified and targeted by a team of ruthless assassins within seconds. It's a similar tale in most places in England, Germany, Italy, Spain etc. Is this because we're a nation of conciliatory, flower-wearing, peace-loving folk? Hardly. It's more a case that the players on the pitch have already beaten the crap out of each other for us, so we just can't be arsed.

Your Ma curing your flu with hot red lemonade.

Although the general topic of this uniquely Irish product was covered in the original 'Stuff' book, this specific use of red lemonade still holds much fondness in our hearts, it seems. Mammies swore by it. She'd warm up a cup of the stuff in a

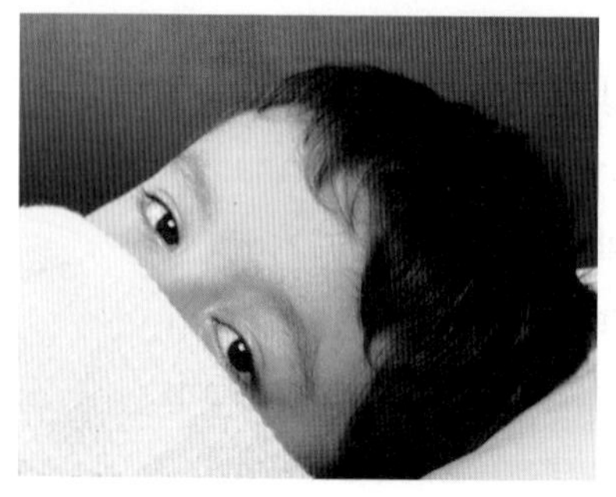

saucepan and gently pour it down her little one's throat, saying, 'this'll have you better in no time at all.' But were there any actual curative values to red lemonade? God only knows what they used in order to make it red. Rusty nails? Or more likely something with a chemical formula like CO3H(S4)-PCH3-(PT8)-UFe18-PS-(Cl)4, which is probably not on the list of approved drugs for the treatment of influenza. Still, it wasn't the worst experience to have considering you could be in school learning the difference between the *modh coinniollach* (the conditional mood) and the *aimsir gnáthláithreach* (present continuous tense).

Pretending you know someone who was in the IRA.

The IRA, it appears, had about a hundred thousand members and not the hard core of about a few thousand that we were told by the politicians. At least that's the conclusion you might reach were you to believe all the claims that are oft heard, mostly in pubs, whispered, that such and such and so and so used to be in the 'Ra' (pronounced Raah). Nobody ever claims to have actually been in the 'Ra' themselves, presumably because such an admission would break some holy sacred vow of eternal silence on penalty of knee-capping or something equally horrific. But if you want to strengthen your extreme nation-alistic credentials, or just to add a touch of mystery or toughness to your persona, a vague allusion to a subversive connection like the 'Ra' is par for the course. And, naturally, it is essential always to refer to the 'Ra' as such, and not as the 'IRA', as only uncool outsiders do this.

These great patriots also usually have certain common traits, like thinking the Land League is a

Gaelic Football tournament, that The Flight of the Wild Geese is a TV program narrated by David Attenborough and that Daniel O'Connell is a country and western singer from Donegal.

Tribunals.

Us? Love tribunals? Do you jest, sir? Are you kidding? Are ye bleedin' wonky in de head, or wha? We, as individual Irish men and women may detest and abhor tribunals, but when have we ever mattered?

But the state of Ireland absolutely loves them, adores them, worships them, which is one of the reasons the state of Ireland is in the state it is. And the bunch of cute hoors who run the state were elected by us, so surely they represent our hopes, wishes and aspirations? Well, only in some mythical Lala land.

Thus we have the McCracken Tribunal, the Moriarty Tribunal, the Mahon Tribunal etc, each lasting the same time as it geologically takes coal to turn into diamond.

And there is a small minority of people who genuinely love tribunals, consisting principally of the people who get paid by them and the people who eternally avoid paying any consequences for their distinctly iffy actions. Members of Ireland's legal profession are our country's principal tribunal-lovers. This is because, collectively, in the last decade they've been paid so much between the various tribunals that they could start their own space program. Perhaps that's it? All our lawyers are planning to fly to Mars. We can only hope.

The other main tribunal-lovers are our elected representatives. You see, in every other country in the western world, what they do when someone is up to dodgy dealings is that they arrest them, try them before a court and, if found guilty, throw the bastards in prison. This is much more satisfactory on many levels. Firstly, the great unwashed, that's us, enjoy intense satisfaction at seeing the smug, illicitly rich gougers thrown behind bars. Secondly, a trial costs a lot less than a tribunal – a comparison would be the difference between buying a tin of Bachelors Beans as opposed to a Gulfstream IV private jet. And lastly, the process would only take a couple of years as opposed to what feels like an eternity.

So why is it that we have tribunals which only have inquisitorial powers and other countries kick the arses of the corrupt into the slammer? Common sense provides the answer. Our great leaders would basically see that as akin to turkeys voting for Christmas. They don't want to create a culture where their fellow politicians and their cronies, whichever party they are associated with, are arrested, just in case the Gardai come battering down *their* door in the middle of the night. They don't want any detectives digging around in *anyone's* murky past, because you never know what they might unearth – when they chopped up the metaphorical body, lots and lots of people each buried a bit in their own back yard. There is also the fact that if the Gardai trap one cute hoor in a corner, he'll probably squeal like a rat.

So, instead, we have tribunals. Which at least provide us with the legal framework openly to call senior, once eminent politicians things like 'ye manky lousy bolloxy shitehawk traitor'. It's an expensive bit of slagging, but that's as good as we're ever going to get from Leinster House.

Irish Rashers.

A few years back, a team of researchers with nothing better to do in Leeds University spent one thousand hours testing seven hundred variations on the 'traditional British bacon sandwich'. This proved a couple of things. One is that British public servants are just as good at ours at wasting taxpayers' money. The other is that if you need a team of researchers working for months on end to discover a tasty bacon sandwich, then British bacon must be really wojus. Any half-decent Irish rasher, on the other hand, will make a glorious rasher sandwich.

Indeed, the word ‘rasher’ most likely comes from the Irish word ‘rásúr’ meaning ‘razor’ (that’s another one to add to the *cúpla focal*!), as in, the bacon is cut with a type of razor and, relative to the lump of meat, is razor thin. A couple of Irish rashers slapped between two slices of buttered batch loaf is surely among Ireland’s greatest creations, among our gifts to the world, ranking up there with the Book of Kells and *Ulysses*.

There is a particular way to eat the Irish rasher sambo, and, unless you have grease running down your chin and your mouth is jammers with bits of semi-masticated rasher fat and crumbling bread, you’re not doing it properly.

You see, we have really special pigs in Ireland.

Beginning a sentence with 'yeah no'.

Example 1: 'Are you goin' for a pint?'

'Yeah no, have to take the wife to see feckin' 'Mamma Mia'.'

Example 2: 'Will ye have me turnips delivered by tomorrow?'

'Yeah no, tomorrow, maybe, no, I don't know. De weather's been brutal.'

Example 3: 'Does my bum look big in this?'

'Yeah no, no, of course not, it looks, eh, thin, eh, round, eh great, I mean.'

All fine examples of Ireland's collective inability to give a definitive answer to a question. See, we don't like absolute answers like 'Yes' and 'No' because they don't leave us with any options, and we always like to keep open the possibility

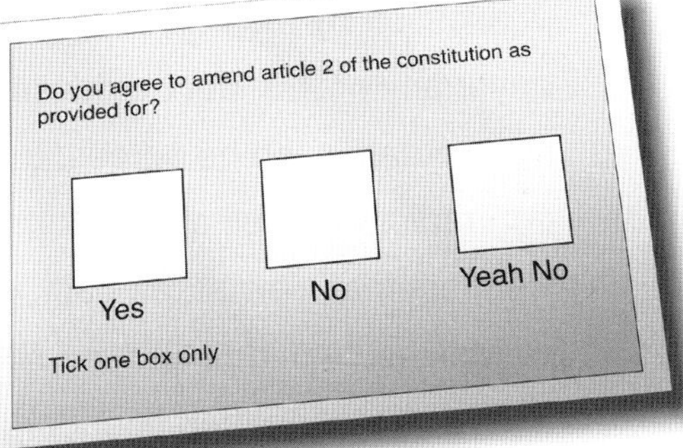

of changing our minds. (*see also* 'Saying 'Naaa' instead of 'No'.)

Take Example 1 above. No Irishman or woman could blatantly refuse the possibility of going for a pint as that would rail against the very core of our being, so in this case, despite the fact that going for a pint is impossible without suffering severe bodily contusions, the man feels it is important to keep open that remote, slim hope. You never know, the wife might break her ankle or 'Mamma Mia' might be cancelled due to heavy snowfalls or something, leaving the chap free to go for a pint.

Example 2 demonstrates how we employ 'yeah no' in our business dealings. The farmer knows with absolute certainty that he won't be delivering the turnips on Thursday because the tractor broke down, his wife left him and his farm has been re-possessed by the bank. Of course he can't tell the buyer any of this, but he doesn't want to damage his reputation, so he agrees, then a moment later contradicts himself as the horror story that is his life rears into view at the back of his mind. Having established a middle ground somewhere between 'yes' and 'no' he then flounders around, hoping the bastard will piss off, finally offering a feeble excuse as to why he cannot give any commitment.

Example 3 demonstrates how we Irish use 'yeah no' as a means of making a point in a way that doesn't offend too greatly, yet still communicates key information. When his wife twirls around in her new dress and proffers her rear end for inspection, her husband immediately thinks, 'Holy shite it's fuckin' massive! I've seen factory ships with smaller arses.' Naturally, he can't say this, but at the same time the horror of what he is witnessing won't allow him in all conscience to lie blatantly, so he mutters 'yeah', then survival instinct kicks in and he follows it with 'no' and a series of pathetic 'complimentary' grunts. This may be sufficient to appease his wife but at the same time will have planted a tiny seed of doubt in her mind, and for the ensuing weeks she will be walking around wondering if, from behind, she looks like she has two exercise balls in her knickers.

The examples above clearly demonstrate that the 'yeah no' construction plays a vital role in Irish inter-personal relationships and is a key component of our national communication skill set.

Giving surnames to our pets.

This may not be an exclusively Irish thing, but it is quite common to be out for a stroll in Ireland and hear some oul' wan yelling out:

'Rufus McDonagh, come here at once, Rufus, or there'll be no dinner for you this evening. Rufus McDonagh!'

The poor mutt hears this as:

'Rufus %^$£%(**%@ Rufus (8^%$¢§¨¶#€º¨¶ˆ§¢¢#§ Rufus 6¶§¢¢ª8¶.'

Addressing our pets as 'Brandy Murphy', Felix O'Shaughnessey and 'Winston Vaughan-Kelly' (Spaniel from Foxrock) is our way of making our beloved pets more human, more a part of the family, although it's unlikely another member of your family might lick his or her own groin area in front of your dinner guests.

67 Being bleakly pessimistic.

Who can blame us for being pessimistic? That great Irishman Oscar Wilde defined a pessimist as one who, when he has a choice of two evils, chooses both. That sums up Ireland for most of the last hundred years. Our two evils came in the form of church and state, the two most influential powers in our lives. It turns out that everything they told us (and we believed) was based on lies, hypocrisy, selfishness, greed, and the unbridled pursuit of power. In the centuries before that we had famine, invasions and massacres, which contributed a little to an air of gloom over the country. Is there any reason we shouldn't be cynical about the future? That's if we have a future, which, in all likelihood, we don't. We're probably all banjaxed

for the rest of our lives. It is safe to say that Irish people feel badly when we feel good because we're afraid we'll feel worse when we feel better.

But on a lighter note, how would you like to hear a joke about an Irish pessimist? Oh, never mind, it's doubtful that you would as the joke is probably shite anyway and you won't like it, so really, what's the point?

68 Telling others that they could have gotten something much cheaper.

Two women meet for a cup of coffee and one displays the top she's just bought for €29.99. The other smiles, pretends to admire the garment and then shakes her head mournfully. 'It's lovely, but I saw those last week for €19.99.' The other woman's smile vanishes as she tries to stuff the top back into the bag, thinking 'What would that oul' geebag know anyway?'

A guy in a factory announces to his colleague that he's just gotten a great deal on a two-week package trip to Majorca. His pal listens, apparently fascinated, then says, '*How much* did you say you paid? You know you could have gotten the same trip for a lot less if you'd gone through London and then rented an apartment via such and such a website.' Suddenly the prospect of sunning his arse and getting pissed in Majorca for a fortnight doesn't sound so great. It's like the sun has gone behind a cloud.

We've all been there. We're all guilty. We've all been victims.

There are several factors at play behind this annoying habit of ours. The first is actually genuine, in that we all know that Ireland is one massive rip-off. It's as though, besides the tax break known as the Artists' Exemption, the government also created another tax break called the Rip-Off Artists' Exemption, and, as a result, countless thousands of the bastards came to live here. So there is that genuine concern whenever you buy something that you're being screwed, which you probably are.

Then there's the pessimism factor (*see also* 'Being bleakly pessimistic'). Even if we don't know for certain that the item or service could be bought somewhere else cheaper, we automatically assume it could have been, as that's our 'glass half empty' nature. All of Irish society, we think, is based on screwing somebody for something. So it's obvious, no matter what you've bought, you've must have been screwed, you poor innocent gobshite.

Finally there's the begrudgery factor, a subject specifically dealt with in the first 'Stuff' book. We hear about our colleague's prospective holiday or see our friend's new purchase and we think, what a jammy scumbag! Why can't I ever find a top like that for a few euro? How come that lazy gouger can afford two weeks in Majorca when all I get is a bollixy week in the pissing rain in Kerry? I'll show him. I'll take the wind out of that little sleeveen's sails!

And you see this book you're reading? You probably could have gotten it for half the price in the bookshop down the road.

Bungalows.

There are about half a million one-off houses in Ireland, mostly in the form of bungalows. That's enough to house almost half of the entire population. Currently, this vast stock of buildings provides accommodation for about the same number of people it takes to fill the snug in Doheny & Nesbitt's pub in Dublin's Baggot Street. Ironically, one of the arguments for building all these bungalows is usually proffered by cute hoor local politicians who thunder that 'Rural people have the right to build homes in the locality in which they grew up'. If that's the case, why in the name of Jaysus are all the houses empty?

The architectural style of the Irish bungalow may be interesting and varied. It may be Edwardian, Georgian, Romanesque, Spanish Colonial, Tudor,

Palladian, Neo-Byzantine or Baroque, to mention but a few styles. And they're all in the one building. Seriously. A typical Irish bungalow has Romanesque pillars as you enter, Tudor ceilings, Georgian windows upstairs, Victorian bay windows downstairs, Palladian wings, stuck on bricks, crazy paving, Spanish roof tiles and two giant plaster eagles atop outsized pillars at the head of the driveway. It will then have a name like 'Baile an Iolar' (Home of the Eagle) or 'Tearmann an Mairnéalach' (The Sailor's Refuge) even if it's 100km from the sea.

The average Irish bungalow looks like the architectural version of Frankenstein's monster, only worse, as instead of assembling the monster with human body parts, the mad scientist has used limbs and brains from an assortment of different animals, and then when it was finished he called it 'Peadar'. Our levels of bad taste know no bounds.

But if you really want to experience the crazed, insane Irish love affair with the bungalow, take a drive along the west coast, top to bottom. It looks like a giant spacecraft flew overhead, scattering enormous handfuls of bungalows randomly over the scenic landscape like they were confetti. One here. One there. One facing this way. One facing that. One looking at the gable end of another. One with six bedrooms. One with two. One white. The next green. The next fake stone. The next pink.

But the most striking thing of all, the creepiest thing, is that when you walk around among the madness, there is utter silence. No doors open and close. No children play in the gardens. No cars sit in the driveways. No voices shatter the silence. It's like the population has been wiped out by a horrible plague or an alien death ray.

See, most of these bungalows are actually owned by the bank because eejits had them built during the 'boom' and now can't afford to pay the mortgage. Those that aren't empty are only visited for a couple of weeks a year, when people come to get away from it all and flee to Connemara or somewhere so they can spend some time enjoying the view of the deserted concrete jungle they can see from their window.

County councillors, planners and parish pump politicians of Ireland: This is your legacy.

You must be *so* proud.

Going for a few pints after Mass.

There is a large section of the population of Ireland who do this, eh, religiously, every Sunday. In fact, it's one of the best reasons to go to Mass. Correction. For many, it's the *only* reason to go to mass. This is why so few practicing Catholics venture from their beds before 11am on a Sunday so they can catch an early Mass. Sure then they'd have to wait for ages for the local to open. No, the receiving of the sacrament must never be pre-noon, so you can go directly into the pub without wasting any precious time.

20 seconds after 12.30 Mass

When the priest says, 'The Mass is ended, go in peace to love and serve the Lord', many of those in the congregation actually hear, 'The pub is opened, go and get pissed 'cause I know you're feckin' bored'.

Shure that communion wafer'd put a fierce thirst on ye.

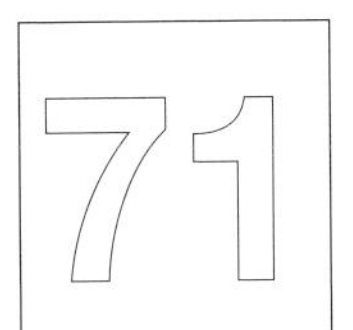

Yokes.

Overseas visitors are often left scratching their heads at our apparent addiction to yokes. They hear us discussing yokes constantly, pointing to yokes, eating yokes, asking for yokes, even snogging yokes, but they've never actually seen a yoke themselves. They go looking for them, asking tour guides where will they find a yoke, can they visit a yoke, how big is a yoke?

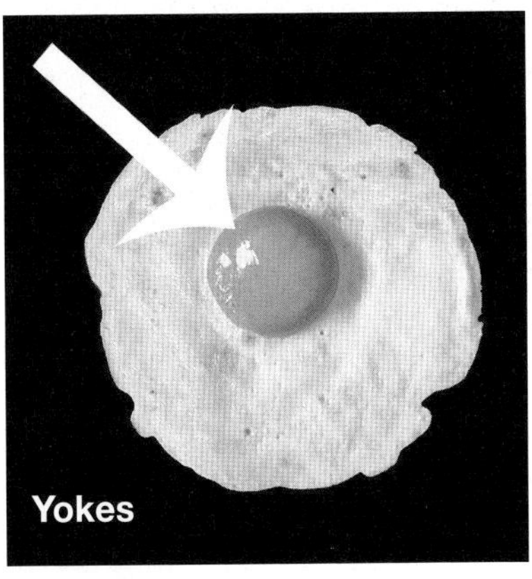
Yokes

Some examples of the prevalence of the yoke in our society:

'Can I borrow that big yoke?

'She's got a fine pair of yokes on her.'

'I'd love one of those yokes, the ones with the yokes on top.'

'That Mary is a right yoke when she's pissed.'

'Where's the yoke that ye need te open this yoke?'

See? We're obsessed by yokes. They're everywhere.

Foreign readers should be aware that a yoke is not the yellow part of the egg, well not specifically, as that may also be a yoke. Understand? Neither is a yoke the wooden bit of an old plough. Well, it can be, but it's not exclusively, as although that specific yoke might be referred to as a yoke, it doesn't work the other way around. There you go. The mystery of the Irish yoke explained in simple terms. Now, time to head down to the yoke for a yoke or two. Might even have a packet of yokes.

99 ice cream cones.

You can still hear the sound of the ice cream van pulling up in your street outside, playing 'Greensleeves' or 'You are my Sunshine' on a gigantic banjaxed music box that has been fed through the van's gammy loud-speakers, which distort it so much that birds who happen to be within earshot fall dead from the sky. Yet to you it's the sound of magic, the possibility of one of life's greatest experiences: the 99 Ice Cream Cone on a summer's evening. You immediately rush to the kitchen and beg the Mammy for money to buy a cone, and after telling you, 'feck off', because she's 'not made of money', she eventually relents just for a bit of peace and quiet. You rush out into the road and observe that a queue of about one hundred and sixty-seven children is already snaking around the corner, each salivating at the prospect of a 99.

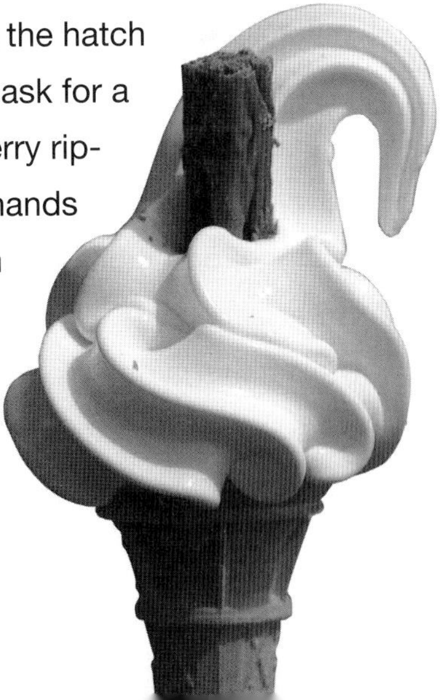

An hour later you reach the hatch in the side of the van and ask for a large 99 cone with raspberry ripple. The man with grotty hands serves up your order from a machine that looks like a prop from a 1950's movie version of 'Dr. Who and the Daleks', gently moving the cone in a tiny spiralling motion and then peaking it off perfectly so it looks like a miniature Mount Everest. He then grabs a half a Cadbury's Flake from a box filled with what look like the flakes that Cadburys dumped in the skip at the back of the factory, and he jams this deep into the soft, yielding body of the ice cream. This work of culinary art is completed with a long squeeze of raspberry sauce from a plastic bottle that still bears part of a label reading 'Jeyes Fluid'.

But none of that matters. Hygiene and food poisoning and bowel surgery are far from your ten-year-old mind. In fact, your entire world has been reduced to three things: your eyes, your beautiful 99 ice cream cone and your gob. Ten minutes of heaven follow, and as the ice cream eventually begins to disappear, you break off the bottom of the cone and scoop up a little ice cream, then detach a sliver of flake and insert it into your own mini creation. For a moment you have recreated the masterpiece in its entirety, albeit a miniature. You swallow this in one glorious bite. Then you stick your tongue down into the cone to scoop out the last remaining bits, which finally leaves you with just a bit of soggy wafer, which you devour in two seconds.

The van pulls away. 'Greensleeves' blares from the speakers and the local dogs wail, and then the van turns a corner and is gone. Irish childhood moments didn't come much better…

73 That St Brendan really discovered America.

Columbus me arse. He was only a thousand years late. Because, as we all know for certain here in Ireland, our own St Brendan beat the Genoa native to it in the sixth century, setting out from Kerry and landing in Newfoundland about seven years later. It took an Englishman, Tim Severin, to prove it could have been done. He constructed a replica boat made of ox hides and Irish ash and followed in

Brendan's wake, landing in Newfoundland in 1977, which gave us the basis for sticking our tongues out to the Italians, Spanish and Portugese, and singing 'Na na nana na'. (Not to mention the Norwegians, who claim that Leif Ericson discovered America around the year 999, a mere 450 years or so after Brendan.) Although he didn't know it at the time, St Brendan would be the first of about fifty million Irish who would take the same route down the years, although, unlike the saint, most of them didn't bother their backsides making the return journey.

Using the phrase 'Ah would you go 'way outta dat!' to express modesty.

We love to think of ourselves as a modest people, not ones to blow our own trumpet too loudly etc. Or at least we used to. This was most commonly expressed when we responded to any compliment by smiling shyly, dropping our eyes and saying 'Ah would ye go 'way outta dat!'

Our false modesty of the past is a vanishing thing, however, as back in the day it used to be considered boastful or even sinful to parade your achievements. But thanks to the excesses of the Celtic Tiger, it has long since become *de rigueur* to make public displays of your 'successes', such as when you see some gobshite who formerly couldn't afford to own a spare pair of jocks arriving in his local pub wearing an Armani suit, or some stupid wagon screeching into the local supermarket car park in a car that would make James Bond blush.

With the demise of the 'boom years', such nonsense has largely vanished, thanks be to Jaysus, and we're now returning to the good old days of false modesty. In fact, our new found modesty is what really makes us so outstanding.

Father Ted.

When most Irish people under thirty watch 'Father Ted' nowadays they think of it merely as a hilarious comedy show, which it is. But to the generation above them it is much more than that. 'Father Ted' was a break-

Fr. Ted's house on Craggy Island

through event in many respects, not least because up to then – despite our ability to be very humorous on a personal level – Ireland had failed to produce a single television comedy show that might raise even a ghost of a smile. Efforts by RTÉ such as 'Upwardly Mobile' and 'Extra Extra' weren't only unfunny, they were so cringe-inducingly brutal that they made you want to stab yourself in the eyes with a pencil and remove your ears with a hacksaw. Then in 1984 along came a series with a potentially funny and intriguing premise, about two priests and their inept housekeeper. No, not 'Father Ted', but the wojus, *evil* 'Leave it to Mrs O'Brien', which was as funny as a rectal operation without anaesthetic. Finally, blessed relief arrived in 1995 in the form of 'Father Ted', and we've been laughing ever since.

Created by two Irish writers, Arthur Matthews and Graham Linehan, and produced by Channel 4, 'Father Ted' didn't just break new ground, it broke previously hallowed ground. Up to that point, the notion of slagging priests or showing priests behaving in decidedly unpriestly ways, (chasing women, stealing, cheating, getting pissed etc) would have had you condemned from the pulpit, banned, flogged, eviscerated and run out of the country by a mob of placard-waving loonies. And in 1995, Ireland was still very much under the (although waning) influence of the Catholic Church. 'Father Ted' was one of the first signs that we were putting all of that behind us; instead of being scared shitless of the Church, we were breaking our shite laughing at them.

'Father Ted' ended after just three seasons with the tragic death of its star, Dermot Morgan. But will we still be watching it in twenty years? To paraphrase Mrs Doyle: '*We will we will we will we will we will we will we will we will we will we will we will we will we will...*'

The phrase 'Ah sure look it' providing the solution to all bad news.

'Paddy's been cheatin' on me with that slapper Tracey, and he's re-mortgaged the house so he could pay for the wagon's boob job and now I'm after gettin' fired.'

'Ah sure look it, it'll be grand.'

Yes, we Irish have discovered the cure for all traumas, the panacea for all of life's ills. All it takes is a simple phrase of four words, which make absolutely no grammatical sense.

House burned down? Ah sure look it…

New car stolen? Ah sure look it…

Put your life savings into Irish bank shares? Ah sure look it…

Presumably it is our way of saying 'Look on the bright side…', except that even when the bright side is about as bright as coal at midnight, 'Ah sure look it' apparently still provides the answer.

It's great, isn't it?

Ireland has debts of two hundred and fifty billion euro. Ah sure look it…

The fact that we're everywhere on the planet.

Nowadays it may be an appalling symptom of our inability to provide a livelihood for a large proportion of our people, and in the past it may have been the tragic result of terrible catastrophes like the Famine, but the fact is that we think it's bleedin' deadly having eighty million or so people around the planet who are either Irish or of Irish descent. And we're all over the shop: Britain, America, Australia, Canada, Argentina, South Africa, Germany, Brazil, France, New Zealand, Kyrgystan (well, maybe not that one). It's particularly great when you're looking for cheap accommodation when you go on holiday.

And don't we feel proud when we see Irish names written so large into the history of so many of those countries. Irish presidents, scientists, military leaders, writers, business leaders, sportsmen, you name it, have all left their mark around the globe, which is great because we need as many friends as we can get, especially now that we're broke.

If only we could convince all these Irish people to start sending money back to the 'ould country' like they used to in the old days, we'd be able to tell the ECB and the IMF to go and feck off.

Going to Mass just to check out the talent.

Nothing to do with the demise of the Catholic Church, as this has been going on in Ireland for centuries. Where else can you get the entire local community jammed into the same room, allowing the boys to peruse a multiplicity of arses while the priest drones on about mortal sins and impure thoughts? Communion was always considered a particularly good opportunity for men and women alike to get a good gawk at the talent on offer. As he/she receives the host they have to turn and walk directly down the aisle towards your lustful eyes, affording you a great view and allowing you to check out every feature from head to toe, and especially the bits in between.

After communion it was just a question of praying that you'd get off with the object of your fancies. And then if you were really lucky you'd have to go to confession the following week, and the bigger the penance, the luckier you'd have been. You just can't beat Irish logic.

An bhfuil cead agam dul amach...?

Our fondness for using the '*cúpla focal*' has been a recurring theme in the previous topics, but this phrase is a particular favourite because it is the single longest sentence of unbroken Irish that most of us can speak. The phrase in its entirety reads:

'An bhfuil cead agam dul amach go dtí an leithreas, más é do thoil é?'

Quite a mouthful, but most of us can reel it off as easily as we'd say 'go and ask me arse'. It is a very handy phrase if you want to impress foreigners with your multi-lingualism, and when they ask what it means, you can just make up any oul' shite. An Irish Carlsberg commercial from a few years back employed this device, where a bunch of Irish lads in a foreign country were seen trying to charm the knickers off a load of foreign beauties by spouting various Irish phrases and words, including the above, and telling them that it was Irish poetry. It has long been a chat-up device that Irish lads keep in their pocket when they encounter foreign girls.

So ladies, ye of non-Irish stock, beware of Irish bowsies charming you with romantic, magical Gaelic brogue, imagining they're telling you that you are the fairest maiden ever to walk on Ireland's soil and that your eyes are like gemstones glittering in a sea of beauty. What they are actually saying in the case of '*An bhfuil cead agam* etc…' is what every single one of us had to learn in school if we wanted to go and have a pee.

In other words, as he stares deeply into your eyes, he's saying, 'May I go out to the toilet, please?'

80 Giving out about the weather.

We're all weather enthusiasts in Ireland. We're obsessed by the weather. Millions tune in every evening to catch the forecast. You couldn't actually increase Irish weather forecast viewership figures short of Met Éireann announcing that in future all forecasters would appear in the nip, and even then we'd still be as interested in the warm front over the Atlantic as the one on the presenter.

In other countries people pay a cursory glance at the weather forecast, usually because they know that the following week is going to be sunny and warm continuously or else minus ten and snowing continuously. The problem in this part of the world is that you just never can tell. Which is why we're never done whingeing about our weather.

Rain, hail, snow, sunshine, wind, calm, warm, thunder, lightning, fog...and that could just be tomorrow's forecast. Usually though, it's the absence of sunshine in summer that's the biggest pain in the arse. Or to re-phrase that, it's the absence of summer that's the biggest pain in the arse. Trying to plan for a barbeque in Ireland is about as easy as converting the Pope to Islam – in theory it's possible, but extremely unlikely.

But the reality is that we've little to give out about, as it never really gets that bad here. In other countries people emerge from their houses in winter, try and locate their car under the snow with a stick and then proceed to dig it out. Here a light dusting of powdery snow causes a national shutdown and chaotic scenes of a despairing nation, reminiscent of the outbreak of war or some terrible natural disaster like an earthquake. Other countries have storms that tear entire houses from their foundations and hurl them into torrents of fast-flowing mud. Here we cower in our homes if the wind is strong enough to blow over one of our plastic patio chairs, an event which occurs about once every thirty years.

So we really shouldn't be whingeing.

Having said that, Irish weather can probably be summed up by the following brief story. An emigrant rings his brother in Ireland and asks if they had a good summer last year. 'Yeah,' he replies, 'we took the kids for a picnic that day.'

Or, as the comedian Hal Roach put it: 'You know it's summer in Ireland when the rain gets warmer.'

Giving out about Ireland and then defending it like a lunatic when a foreigner insults us.

Besides the weather, we do love to moan endlessly about the country we all love. Brutal, cute hoor politicians, wojus health service, crap transport, corrupt bankers, underworked and overpaid public service, too much tax, the price of a pint, the Catholic Church, the price of petrol, the traffic etc etc etc are the subjects of one long continuous national moanfest. Which is fair enough. We certainly have made a bollox of the place in many regards, and continue to do so. But the thing is, if anyone from beyond these shores dares to whisper a hint of criticism about any aspect of Ireland, we descend en masse upon the unfortunate's head and proceed to metaphorically kick his backside into kingdom come.

A few years ago, Christian Pauls, the German ambassador to Ireland, dared to criticise the place on several fronts, complaining about the dominant position of the Church, the chaotic health service, overpaid politicians and various other things, all stuff we rant about ourselves on a daily basis. So did we shake his hand, clap him on the back? We did in our arse.

Cue a torrent of outrage on the airwaves from furious citizens ranting that Herr Pauls should feck off back to *Das Vaterland* if he doesn't like it here.

The Minister for Foreign Affairs, Dermot Ahern, phoned the German embassy to condemn the 'unbalanced picture', and MEP Gay Mitchell said he was 'shocked' at the comments. Jaysus. What are we like? Why the shock? Didn't he say precisely what we were thinking? That's not the point! The dirty bowsie's got no right to slag us; we're the only ones allowed to do that!

You'll find the same thing on a personal level every day of the week. People who normally spend their drinking hours bemoaning how gammy this is and how banjaxed that is, will defend the place to the hilt in the company of foreign guests. A casual remark by a foreigner about say, the Irish being the litterbugs that we are, and shoulders will immediately be thrown back and affronted expressions will snap into place, before the poor guest is subjected to a verbal attack from several fronts, by the end of which he'll agree that litter isn't such a big deal, that it actually may have its positive side.

So, apparently what we really want is to happily go on moaning about the state of the place to each other, but we want everyone beyond these shores to believe that we reside in some kind of utopian fairyland where nothing ever goes wrong. They also are allowed to say only nice things about us, otherwise our feelings will be hurt, sensitive little souls that we are.

Little wonder that Freud said that we were a race for whom psychoanalysis is of no use whatsoever.

Hey! Who does that Freud gobshite think he is anyway?

Are ye dancin'?

This one will be a mystery to anyone under thirty, but here is the phrase that launched a million marriages, or at least a million gropes behind the dance hall. It was the Irish male's most potent chat-up line for decades. In fact, it was the Irish male's *only* chat-up line for decades. Back in the day when virtually all romance commenced in the local dance hall, or, as times moved on, 'the dishcho', the girls would gather in groups or even on one side of the hall, the boys ranged along the other, casting nervous, lascivious stares across the room.

The hall was illuminated by a mirror ball, a set of coloured lights over the stage, and sometimes, if it was very trendy, by ultra-violet light, which was great if any hint of a girl's bra was visible as it would begin to glow purple and invite closer inspection and much hilarious comment. The lads would stand there for an hour knocking back the Dutch courage and making lewd comments to show how cool and unperturbed they all were. Things like 'That Brigid one's a life support system for a fanny' was a particular favourite, or 'That one's arse is the width of a Mullingar heifer,' was also liked. This of course was all a cover for the terror of possible rejection should they approach one of the ladies.

All the men on one side ...

But eventually enough drink would be taken and someone would venture forth, approaching his prey with as much panache as a one-legged orang utan, and charming the lucky girl with the mesmerising line 'Are ye dancin'? If she didn't fancy him, the unfortunate eejit usually received the reply 'No, it's just the way I'm feckin' standin'!' or 'I'm sittin' at a table drinkin' a vodka and coke. Do I look like I'm bleedin' dancin'?' Alternatively it was the pithier 'No, piss off,' which left little room for doubt.

However, occasionally one of the ladies might decide that she might just be missing out on a potentially big romance leading to marriage and a lifetime of bliss, in which case the correct response was 'Are ye askin'?' 'Yeah, I'm askin' responded the guy, 'Then I'm dancin'' said the girl. If the guy managed to keep the girl dancin' for ten minutes or so, he would then chance his arm for a snog. This often resulted in a knee in the groin, but if successfully snogged back, the guy then progressed to sliding his palms down and clasping a buttock in each hand. If his hands weren't removed, there was a very good chance the pair would be married within six months.

Yes, young folk, these were the strange courtship rituals of days gone by. If you doubt it, go and ask your parents and watch them turn red.

Ah, God be with de days…

If you enjoyed this book you'll love the first *STUFF IRISH PEOPLE LOVE*: The Definitive Guide to the Unique Passions of the Paddies and Murphy & O'Dea's bestselling *Feckin'* collection:

The Feckin' Book of Irish Slang
The Feckin' Book of Irish Sayings
The Feckin' Book of Irish Sex and Love
The 2nd Feckin' Book of Irish Slang
The Fecking Book of Irish Recipes
The Feckin' Book of Irish Songs
The Feckin' Book of Irish Quotations
The Feckin' Book of Irish Insults
The Feckin' Book of Irish Trivia
The Feckin' Book of Everything Irish
The Feckin' Book of Irish History
Now That's What I Call A Big Feckin' Irish Book
The Feckin' Book of Bankers, Builders etc
The Feckin' Book of Irish Stuff